BLESSED MARIE
OF NEW FRANCE

BOOKS BY MARY FABYAN WINDEATT

A Series of Twenty Books

Stories of the Saints for Young People ages 10 to 100

THE CHILDREN OF FATIMA
And Our Lady's Message to the World

THE CURÉ OF ARS
The Story of St. John Vianney, Patron Saint of Parish Priests

THE LITTLE FLOWER
The Story of St. Therese of the Child Jesus

PATRON SAINT OF FIRST COMMUNICANTS
The Story of Blessed Imelda Lambertini

THE MIRACULOUS MEDAL
The Story of Our Lady's Appearances to St. Catherine Labouré

ST. LOUIS DE MONTFORT
The Story of Our Lady's Slave, St. Louis Mary Grignion De Montfort

SAINT THOMAS AQUINAS
The Story of "The Dumb Ox"

SAINT CATHERINE OF SIENA
The Story of the Girl Who Saw Saints in the Sky

SAINT HYACINTH OF POLAND
The Story of the Apostle of the North

SAINT MARTIN DE PORRES
The Story of the Little Doctor of Lima, Peru

SAINT ROSE OF LIMA
The Story of the First Canonized Saint of the Americas

PAULINE JARICOT
Foundress of the Living Rosary & The Society for the Propagation of the Faith

SAINT DOMINIC
Preacher of the Rosary and Founder of the Dominican Order

SAINT PAUL THE APOSTLE
The Story of the Apostle to the Gentiles

SAINT BENEDICT
The Story of the Father of the Western Monks

KING DAVID AND HIS SONGS
A Story of the Psalms

SAINT MARGARET MARY
And the Promises of the Sacred Heart of Jesus

SAINT JOHN MASIAS
Marvelous Dominican Gatekeeper of Lima, Peru

SAINT FRANCIS SOLANO
Wonder-Worker of the New World and Apostle of Argentina and Peru

BLESSED MARIE OF NEW FRANCE
The Story of the First Missionary Sisters in Canada

BLESSED MARIE
OF NEW FRANCE

THE STORY OF THE
FIRST MISSIONARY SISTERS IN CANADA

By
Mary Fabyan Windeatt

Illustrated by
Lili Réthi

TAN BOOKS AND PUBLISHERS, INC.
Rockford, Illinois 61105

Nihil Obstat: Gerard A. Green, S.T.B.
                      Censor Deputatus

Imprimatur: ✠ Francis Cardinal Spellman
                      Archbishop of New York
                      New York
                      July 8, 1958

The Nihil Obstat and Imprimatur are official declarations that a book or pamphlet is free of doctrinal or moral error. No implication is contained therein that those who have granted the Nihil Obstat and Imprimatur agree with the contents, opinions or statements expressed.

ISBN: 0-89555-432-1

Library of Congress Catalog Card No.: 93-61383

Printed and bound in the United States of America.

TAN BOOKS AND PUBLISHERS, INC.
P.O.Box 424
Rockford, Illinois 61105

1994

For
Reverend Paschal Boland, O.S.B.,
Monk of Saint Meinrad Archabbey,
Saint Meinrad, Indiana,
in appreciation of much kindness.

CONTENTS

ACKNOWLEDGMENTS

THE AUTHOR is deeply grateful to Mother Mary of Jesus, O.S.U., Mother Saint George, O.S.U., and Mother Saint Joseph, O.S.U., of the Ursuline Monastery, Quebec, Canada, for their generous help and encouragement in preparing this story of Mère Marie de l'Incarnation. Appreciation is also due the following for the loan of much valuable source material: Reverend Paul-Emile Racicot, S.J., *Propagandiste des Fondateurs de l'Eglise Canadienne,* Montreal, Canada; Reverend Placidus Kempf, O.S.B., and Reverend Adrian Fuerst, O.S.B., monks of Saint Meinrad Archabbey, Saint Meinrad, Indiana; Mother M. Celeste Hanlon, O.S.U., Provincial of the Ursulines of the Roman Union, Kirkwood, Missouri; and Mother M. Claire, O.S.U., Louisville, Kentucky.

BLESSED MARIE
OF NEW FRANCE

CHAPTER 1

THE MOTHER

YOUNG PIERRE DUPLETTE laid three fresh logs atop the small fire on his master's hearth, then glanced hopefully at the white-haired figure bent over a desk in the far corner of the room. Bertrand d'Eschaux, the Archbishop of Tours, was not a man to demand bodily comforts for himself, even on a cold January morning like this one of the year 1631. There was good reason to believe that a special visitor was about to arrive, and a special visitor generally meant not only a bit of decent warmth in the Archbishop's drab study, but wine and cakes as well.

"Monseigneur, is there anything else you'd like?" asked the boy respectfully.

Slowly the old Archbishop rose to his feet and approached the crackling fire. "No, Pierre—unless it is the answers to a few questions."

"And what would they be, Monseigneur?"

"First, do you know anything of Madame Marie Martin?"

"The daughter of Florent Guyart, the baker? The

1

poor woman who lost her husband eleven years ago?"

"The same."

Pierre nodded vigorously. "Oh, yes, Monseigneur! A very holy soul. Whenever I see her praying in church, I always feel as though I'm watching a saint. She's wonderfully kind to the poor, too. And of course a fine mother to her boy."

"Ah, young Claude. By the way, how old is the lad now?"

"Not quite twelve, Monseigneur. And a strange little character, if I may say so."

"Strange?"

"Well, perhaps that's not the word. But everyone knows he ran away to Paris last week because he said he wasn't loved at home. Three days he was gone, too, which almost broke his mother's heart. Can you imagine a normal child doing such a thing?"

The Archbishop smiled. Young Pierre Duplette—serious, hard-working and trustworthy—had been all but a son to him since that fateful day, eighteen years before, when the plague had carried off both the boy's parents.

"Now, Pierre, don't forget it takes all kinds of folk to make a world," he observed mildly. "Claude Martin will find his place someday." Then, suddenly, cocking his ear, he said, "But isn't that the doorbell? Run and answer it like a good soul. I'm expecting a visitor."

Pierre's eyes shone. So, he'd been right after all! "Of course, Monseigneur. I'll go at once. And perhaps you'll be wanting wine and cakes in a little while?"

The Archbishop nodded. "Yes, Pierre. The best wine and cakes in the house."

Alone for a moment, Bertrand d'Eschaux turned from the fire and crossed the room to stand by the window overlooking a rustic shrine to Our Lady in the garden outside. It was a desolate place now, the little shrine, with only a few barren trees and vines for a background. Yet the face of the Virgin's statue was as gracious as in the time of blossoms. Indeed, the outstretched hands suddenly seemed to come alive in the pale January sunlight as though they would bestow upon the Archbishop all manner of priceless treasures.

"Not so much for myself as for another, Holy Virgin," he pleaded silently.

Even as the Archbishop prayed, there came a soft rap at the door. Turning, he saw an attractive woman in her early thirties being ushered into the room by a somewhat bewildered Pierre. So there was a reason behind all those questions, the boy's look plainly said.

Although the newcomer was very simply attired—a black hooded cloak covering a dress of common gray homespun—her smile was as radiant as that of a young girl, and the dark eyes lifted to his own as she came forward to kiss his ring were extraordinarily beautiful.

"*Bonjour*, Madame Martin! How good to see you!"

"*Bonjour*, Monseigneur! How good of you to want to see me!"

When Pierre had left the room, the Archbishop motioned his guest to a chair beside his own close to the fire. "I sent word for you to come, Madame, after hearing what the Prioress of the Ursulines had to tell me yesterday. That was surely good news!"

Madame Martin's slim fingers toyed with the rough folds of her cloak. "Mère Françoise de Saint Bernard, she . . . she told you everything, Monseigneur?"

"She told me that you plan to enter the convent very soon; that your sister and her husband have promised to look after your little boy until he comes of age; and that everything is going to work out well."

In spite of her brave efforts to control them, sudden tears glistened in Madame Martin's dark eyes. "It. . .it's like my beautiful childhood dream come true," she whispered. "And yet at times I'm so frightened, Monseigneur—almost as though the dream were coming true too late. . . ."

The Archbishop leaned forward earnestly. "If anything's troubling you, Madame, why not begin at the beginning and tell me all about it? Maybe I can help you."

"But it would take so long—"

"Nonsense! Today my time is all yours. Come, let's start at the beginning. What's this about a childhood dream coming true?"

So, haltingly at first, then with renewed courage, Madame Martin began to relate her story.

"I was a little girl of seven, Monseigneur, when I dreamed that Our Lord came down through the sky to the schoolyard where I was playing and asked me if I'd be His special friend. So great was the love that came into my heart that right away in my dream I said I would."

"And then?"

"I was so happy afterward that I told everyone of what had happened. No one paid much attention, of course, for it was only a dream, but I didn't mind. It was enough to know that Jesus loved me, and that I loved Him more than anyone or anything in the world."

"So?"

"By the time I was fourteen, I felt that I was called to be a nun. I told this to my mother, who was most kind, but she said I was still very young and that I must think and pray a great deal before making any decision. She was so serious, Monseigneur, that somehow I was led to believe that convent life was not for me. Then, when I was seventeen—"

"Yes?"

"My father decided I ought to marry a silk merchant—Claude Martin. He was so set on the idea, and Claude was such a good young man, that I never dreamed of questioning anything. We were married in just a few weeks. Two years later, when I was nineteen, our little boy Claude was born."

The Archbishop nodded approvingly. It had been a good idea to have Madame Martin tell her story. The tears were gone from her eyes now, and she seemed to be far more at ease.

"And then what happened, my child?"

"Presently our silk business began to fail. This worried my husband so much that soon he became quite ill. I nursed him as well as I could, but he only grew worse. Within six months he was dead, Monseigneur, leaving me penniless, and with a little baby to care for."

"And you just twenty years old? Poor child! What did you do then?"

"For almost two years I lived at home and helped my father with his bakery business. After that I went to live with my older sister Claude and her husband Paul."

"Ah, Madame and Monsieur Buisson?"

"Yes. And how good they've been to my boy and me during the past nine years! We've never wanted for anything."

For a moment the Archbishop was silent, busying himself with adding a fresh log to the fire. But when he turned to Madame Martin, an odd smile was playing about his lips. "Probably you've earned that blessing," he observed dryly. "Doesn't Monsieur Buisson own a thriving transportation business? And don't you practically run it for him?"

"Well—"

"Dozens of vans, carts, horses, drivers, shipments to and from all parts of France—"

"I'm used to the work, Monseigneur."

"Payrolls to meet, bills to be paid, books to be balanced, warehouses to manage—"

"Please, Monseigneur—"

"Merchandise to be accounted for, disputes to be settled—ah, Madame, I've often heard it said that you're down at the river docks until well after midnight whenever a boat comes in."

Madame Martin smiled faintly. "You're making me seem like a martyr," she protested, "when all this work is nothing more than God's will for me. Yet right along I've felt that someday He'd call me to other work. Once my boy was old enough to do without a mother's care, He'd want me to go to some convent to give myself to His service."

"And now you think the time has come?"

"I know it has, Monseigneur. Claude will be twelve in April. And the Ursulines have just agreed to let me try their way of life."

For a moment the Archbishop was thoughtful. What was it Madame Martin had said earlier? *"It's like my beautiful childhood dream come true...and yet at times I'm so frightened...almost as though the dream were coming true too late...."*

"My child," he said finally, "you've scarcely mentioned young Claude's part in all this. That, I'm sure, is what is troubling you. Does the lad know that you plan to leave him for the convent?"

"Not yet, Monseigneur. I haven't had the courage to tell him. But he may suspect some kind of change, for of late the house has been a strange and miserable place. My sister and brother-in-law are so upset about my plans that sometimes they scarcely speak to or look at either of us."

"They don't approve of your being a nun?"

"Oh, no! They say the religious life is for young girls with no responsibilities, not a thirty-one-year-old widow with a fatherless boy to support. Besides, their business is growing very rapidly, and they say I owe it to them to stay on and help."

"Yet yesterday Mère Françoise* told me that the Buissons have agreed to care for Claude!"

"Ah, but only grudgingly. And whenever I think of the poor child's growing up without either of his real parents with him, my heart almost breaks. God is calling me to His service, Monseigneur, and I long to answer the summons. But where am I to find the courage to leave my boy? Where? And when?"

Slowly the old Archbishop rose to his feet and led Madame Martin to the window overlooking the garden. "There," he said gently, pointing to the Virgin's little shrine, "there is a woman who knew how to lose her Son, my child. Ask her for help."

"But—"

"It's hard, of course. Very hard. But when you leave here, you must go at once to Claude and tell him everything. Our Lady will help the little fellow to understand far better than you think."

Upon her return to the Buisson house, Madame Martin went immediately in search of Claude. She found him in his room, pale-faced and woebegone, idly leafing through an old textbook. Removing her cloak, she sat down beside him.

"Darling, what's the trouble?" she asked anxiously. "Don't you feel well?"

The boy's thin mouth tightened. "I . . . I'm all right, Maman."**

---

*"Mère" = French for "Mother." ("Mère" rhymes with "fair.")
**"Maman" = "Mama."

"But you look so unhappy! Wouldn't you like to go outside and play with your little cousin Marie?"

"There's no fun in playing with a four-year-old girl."

"Well, what would you like to do then?"

"Nothing."

"But, Claude—"

Suddenly the boy threw down his book and burst into tears. "Maman, why is everything so different these days?" he sobbed. "Why do people stop talking as soon as they see me, then shake their heads and turn away as though something dreadful were going to happen? There's. . .there's some kind of terrible secret. . . ."

"Now, son—"

"I can't stand it, Maman! I just can't! And while you were gone this morning, I heard Uncle Paul tell Aunt Claude that you've never really loved me!"

A pang shot through the mother's heart as she forced herself to remain calm. What a terrible mistake not to have taken this child into her confidence long ago! No wonder he had run off to Paris last week, bewildered and hurt by all the idle gossip in the Buisson house.

"Darling, listen to me," she said comfortingly. "I love you more than anyone or anything in the world. Can't you believe that?"

"But—"

"And because I love you so much, I'm going to ask you to help me do something very important. No one but you can have a part in this, Claude—not even the wisest or the richest or the greatest person on earth."

Slowly the boy's sobs lessened. "W-what is it?" he choked. "W-what do you mean, Maman?"

"I want you to help me save souls, son—through sacrifice."

"But I don't understand—"

"Listen, dear. Ever since you were a little baby, and even long before that, I've wanted to be a nun. Now, do you think you could let me go away to be an Ursuline? Could you give me permission for that?"

For a long moment Claude stared at his mother, his eyes perplexed and fearful. "Is. . .is that the secret everyone's been trying to keep from me?"

"That's it."

"You mean you want to go away from here and never see me again?"

"Of course not, darling! The Ursuline convent is only a few blocks away. You may come for visits as often as you wish."

"But, Maman—"

"Think, son, what it means when people enter the religious life! In due course all the prayers they offer, all the duties they perform, are given a wonderful new power to save the poor sinners of the world. Wouldn't you be glad for me to have a blessing like that?"

Claude looked uncertainly at the floor. In all his eleven years he had never known such a situation as this. Maman, from whom he had so often asked one permission or another, was now asking a permission from him! And not only was she waiting for his decision, millions of others must be waiting for it, too, in that mysterious world of sinners with which Maman seemed to be so concerned. . . .

Slowly the boy raised his eyes. "I. . .I guess it'll be all right for you to go to the convent," he said finally, and his voice was very small and low. "I guess you'll do a lot of good there, Maman."

Madame Martin's heart all but broke. How she longed to press this solemn-faced youngster to her breast, to pour out her love for him in tender words and caresses. But since that might lead to tears, she contented herself with tracing the Sign of the Cross upon Claude's forehead as he knelt at her feet.

"Son, you've made me very proud and happy," she whispered. "Now, shall we go and find Uncle Paul and Aunt Claude and tell them what you've just told me? They'll be so relieved to hear how brave you've been!"

However, the Buissons were disappointed at Claude's reaction to his mother's plans. The loss of a worker who had been so useful to them during the past nine years was hard to bear, and they made no effort to hide their feelings.

"Marie, how can you hope to be an Ursuline at your age?" demanded Paul Buisson impatiently. "For one thing, your health won't stand the strain. For another, it's foolish for an experienced businesswoman to shut herself away in a convent. Why, just think of all the good you could do if you stay in the world!"

Madame Buisson nodded tearfully. "That's right, Marie. Think of the dozens of our own workmen you've helped to return to the Sacraments."

"But once you're gone, who's to see that they don't slip back again into their old ways?"

"And their wives and families with them?"

Madame Martin smiled. "You two have forgotten one important thing," she said thoughtfully, "God's will. To the best of my knowledge, He wants me to join the Ursulines. Therefore, nothing else matters."

Marie Martin's father, old Florent Guyart, objected to his daughter's religious vocation as vigorously as did her sister and brother-in-law. But in spite of all family arguments, a strange little procession set out through the streets of Tours for the Ursuline convent on the morning of January 25, 1631, the feast of the conversion of Saint Paul. First came little Marie Buisson, bearing her aunt's large crucifix. Next came the Buissons, then Florent Guyart, Marie Martin herself, Dom Raymond (the priest who had long been her confessor), Claude and several friends and neighbors. Nearly everyone was weeping save Madame Martin. Her heart was heavy, of course, at the impending separation from her son, but she forced herself to appear in good spirits and to walk briskly.

"Dear Lord, don't let me weaken!" she murmured. "Don't let me see those tears in Claude's eyes."

A moment later, as the group reached the convent and the heavy wooden doors swung wide, the struggle was over. Not trusting herself to say good-by, Madame Martin merely smiled at her dear ones, knelt for Dom Raymond's blessing, then resolutely

A STRANGE LITTLE PROCESSION SET OUT
FOR THE URSULINE CONVENT.

crossed the threshold into the cloister. There the Prioress and her community were awaiting her with open arms.

As she looked at all the eager faces about her, suddenly it seemed to Marie Martin that she had known this new family all her life. Of course the Prioress, Mère Françoise de Saint Bernard, had been her dear friend for some time, but now the others—the bright-eyed little novices, the Sisters who worked in kitchen, garden and laundry, the infirm and aged ones whom one of these days God would reward with eternal joy—all were at once immeasurably dear to her.

"Dear Lord, how can I thank You?" she prayed silently. "At last I've come home!"

The next morning Soeur Marie* (for thus she would be known until she received the habit) was even happier. What peace and joy within these convent walls where everyone was dedicated to God's service! Of course it was a pity that her twenty-eight companions in the novitiate—the oldest was only sixteen—had somehow decided that she had been a very important person in the world and so must now be treated with unusual consideration. For instance, a moment ago—

"I'll wash that window, Soeur Marie," one little novice had insisted. "That kind of work is too hard for you."

"And I'll mop the floor," another had put in cheerfully. "After all, you shouldn't undertake too

---

*"Soeur" = French for "Sister."

much in your first few days here."

"Oh, no, Sister! Especially not at your age."

As she set herself to the one task which had been allowed her—the dusting of a few chairs—Soeur Marie could scarcely keep from laughing. If only these little Sisters could know the amount of work which she had handled for her brother-in-law, even to the unharnessing, feeding and bedding down of some fifty truck horses at night! But of course these little novices meant well, and it would never do to hurt their feelings. A few words to the Novice Mistress, and the problem would surely be solved.

Even as she was reflecting upon all this, a bell sounded in the corridor. At once pails were carried off to be emptied, mops and dusters put away, aprons doffed, veils and habits straightened.

"Soeur Marie, we have special prayers in the chapel now," whispered the senior novice. "Please come and take your place in line."

As she started from the room with the others, Soeur Marie's eyes sparkled with joy. It was so good to be here, to know that she had given herself to God as best she could, and that now all that mattered was to obey the holy Rule in all things!

But a moment later, as she took her place in the chapel, she suddenly felt her blood run cold. Far away in the distance was the heart-rending wail of a familiar little voice:

"Maman, Maman, where are you?"

Soeur Marie turned pale. Surely that couldn't be Claude! Yet the brief stir among the young nuns kneeling beside her, the swift glances of sympathy, were proof enough.

"Hail Mary, full of grace, the Lord is with thee," intoned the Novice Mistress calmly.

"Blessed art thou amongst women, and blessed is the fruit of thy womb, Jesus," responded the novices.

"Incline unto my aid, O God."

"O Lord, make haste to help me."

"Glory be to the Father, and to the Son, and to the Holy Ghost."

"As it was in the beginning, is now, and ever shall be. . . ."

Soeur Marie's head drooped. Even above this earnest chorus of prayer she could still hear her child's frantic crying—nearer now, and more intense:

"Maman, Maman, where are you? I want you back!"

CHAPTER 2

THE DREAM

WHEN PRAYERS were over, the understanding Prioress quickly came in search of Soeur Marie. Yes, Claude had been crying his heart out at the convent gate, she said, but the portress had taken him into the parlor. Now he was feeling much better.

"We gave him some little almond cakes," she said to Soeur Marie, "and they stopped the tears. Do come and have a visit with him."

Soeur Marie scarcely knew what to say. "Mother, how can I thank you?" she burst out. "Or tell you how ashamed I am—"

The Prioress smiled. "There, now, it's only natural that the boy should miss you on your first full day away from home," she said kindly. "Mark my words, though, he'll soon get over being lonely."

Alas for such a hope! That same afternoon young Claude Martin was back again at the convent, pounding on the big wooden gate and crying as though his heart would break. In vain Soeur Marie begged him to offer his loneliness for some poor sinner.

"I don't know any poor sinners!" he sobbed. "Maman, why don't you come home? We miss you so much!"

For weeks the same state of affairs continued. Either alone or in the company of other little boys, some armed with sticks and stones, Claude came to the convent to demand his mother's return. On one occasion he even managed to slip into the cloister through a door which some workmen had left open and then make his way to the refectory where the nuns were at dinner.

"Give me back my mother!" he stormed. "Give her back right now!"

Soeur Marie stared in horror. Surely this was the end of everything! For how could the community continue to endure such annoying disturbances? Certainly they would never give her the habit on March 25, as she had hoped and planned...

However, Soeur Marie's good friend and confessor, Dom Raymond, aided by the Archbishop, decided to ask the Jesuits in Rennes to accept young Claude as a pupil at their boarding school.

"God be praised!" exclaimed the Archbishop, when he heard that the plea had been successful. "I'm sure Claude will do very well with the Jesuits. He's not a bad little fellow at heart, just confused and lonely."

Dom Raymond shrugged. "I'm surprised to hear that the Buissons plan to pay his tuition," he observed dryly.

"Ah, Father, a matter of conscience, that. Perhaps they're beginning to feel guilty for their part in this whole affair."

"Monseigneur! You can't mean they put Claude up to all his tricks!"

"In part, Father. Monsieur Buisson had to hire two men at high wages to do the work which his sister-in-law formerly did for nothing. Somehow he decided that if Claude could be led to make a real nuisance of himself at the convent—"

"The nuns would send Madame Martin home?"

"Exactly. Then things could be as they were before. But what a mistake on the poor man's part! The Ursulines are more than pleased with Madame Martin, and she with them."

True enough. On March 25, 1631, Soeur Marie was allowed to receive the habit of the Order of Saint Ursula. She was also told that henceforth she would be known as Soeur Marie de l'Incarnation, and that if all went well she would make her final vows in two years' time.

Two years seemed an eternity to the eager novice, but the days succeeded one another with incredible swiftness. Never had Soeur Marie been so happy. Yet there were trials, too—times when God seemed so very far away that it was difficult to believe He existed, much less to want to give her whole life to Him.

"Ah, that's only the devil trying to discourage you," said the Novice Mistress kindly. "He uses that little trick a million times a day, Sister, inside the cloister and out. But there's a way to make that same little trick earn a wonderful grace."

Soeur Marie hesistated. "There is, Mother? But how?"

"By telling God that we believe and hope in Him, even though that seems impossible; by telling God that we love Him, even though that seems a waste of time. Ah, Soeur Marie, little prayers like that can spoil all the devil's plans and win for us the very virtues we think we'll never have!"

Deep in her heart Soeur Marie had always known this truth, but it was very consoling to have it impressed upon her by such an experienced religious as the Novice Mistress. Now, perhaps, if she mentioned another trial that had come to her of late—

"What is it, my dear?" asked the Novice Mistress, reading her thoughts. "What else is troubling you?"

Soeur Marie took a deep breath. "Just this, Mother. Sometimes I'm tempted to think that God doesn't want me to spend all my days in Tours. He—well, He has work for me elsewhere."

"*What?*"

"I know it sounds strange, Mother, especially when I love this place so much. But that's the way it is."

The Novice Mistress stared in amazement. There was complete honesty in the dark eyes searching her own, unmarred by the slightest trace of pride. Yet how unusual for a mere novice to make such a statement! Ursuline nuns generally lived and died in the convent that had received them.

"Sister, that sounds like another trick of the devil to get you to waste your time in idle daydreaming," she said finally. "Put away such nonsense as best you can, and don't worry about anything."

Soeur Marie seemed relieved. "Of course, Mother," she said cheerfully. "That's just what I'll do."

Yet, in the months that followed, Soeur Marie de l'Incarnation found it next to impossible to obey the advice of the Novice Mistress. For the present it did seem that God wished her to remain in Tours. But surely, when she had made her final vows, the way would be opened up to her.

"Dear Lord, whatever You wish," she prayed silently. "Just keep me close to You always. And make a saint of my boy."

There was good reason to pray for Claude. In the summer of 1632 the Jesuits dismissed him from their school in Rennes and sent him back to Tours. His mother might be a good religious, they said, but the lad himself was the shiftless sort, with not the slightest interest in his studies. A pity, of course, that his uncle Paul Buisson had recently died. Still, his Aunt Claude could surely make some kind of a home for him.

Surprisingly enough, Madame Buisson received her nephew with open arms, and in a few short weeks the boy was a changed person. He no longer seemed to mind his mother's being in the convent. Indeed, when she made her final vows on January 25, 1633, he insisted on being present at the ceremony. More than that, he began to show an interest in returning to school—this time to the Jesuits in Orléans.

"If they'll have me, I'll really try to study hard," he promised.

Soeur Marie was overjoyed. Claude would soon be fourteen. How wonderful if her many prayers and sacrifices for him were about to be rewarded, and he was really going to settle down at last!

"Well, we'll surely do our very best for Claude," said Père Georges de la Haye, the rector of the Jesuit school in Orléans, who happened to be passing through Tours and had come to see Soeur Marie at the convent. "But of course we won't stand for any nonsense, Soeur Marie. The boy will have to obey the rules and keep up with his classmates, or else be dismissed. Does he understand that?"

Soeur Marie nodded eagerly. "I'm sure he does, Father."

Happily Claude did so well in his new school that by Christmas of the year 1634 he had endeared himself to everyone there. The good news was received with delight at the Ursuline convent where his mother had recently been promoted to the post of assistant Novice Mistress of the community. Henceforth she would be known not as Soeur Marie but as Mère Marie de l'Incarnation.

One night shortly after her new appointment, as she drifted into a light sleep, Mère Marie had a curious dream. She seemed to have just completed a long sea voyage in company with a fair-haired young woman whom she had never seen before. Now they were landing in a strange and mountainous country, heavily shrouded in mist. Hand in hand they went ashore and began to climb a rugged path that led up the side of a sheer rock. Here they met an old man, clothed in flowing garments, who seemed to be the guardian of the country. Though he smiled in a most friendly fashion, he did not speak. He merely pointed to a small church farther up the rock, as if to indicate that there was their goal.

Nearby were other and more stately buildings, but Mère Marie paid them scant heed. She and her companion must reach that beautiful little church at once! So without delay they crossed an open courtyard of white marble tiles, with joinings of vivid scarlet, and struggled upward to God's house on the rock. A moment later they saw that it, too, was of white marble, and that in a niche above the entrance was a life-sized statue of Our Lady, seated on a throne and holding her Child. From where they stood, however, they had only a side view of the statue.

For some time Mère Marie and her companion in the dream stared in silent wonder. Who had built this beautiful little church in the wilderness? Then Mère Marie's gaze turned downward to the country-side through which they had just passed—a vast and terrifying place of rock and forest, of mountains and valleys—half lost in threatening clouds and shadows. Shivering, she suddenly had a great desire to see Our Lady's statue face to face. Dropping her companion's hand, she hurried forward to a place directly beneath the niche above the church's entrance. Here, standing on tiptoe, she could almost touch the statue.

For a moment Mère Marie gazed in delight. How beautiful Our Lady was, how young—no more than

ALL AT ONCE THE FIGURES WERE OF
REAL FLESH AND BLOOD!

fifteen or sixteen years of age! But. . .but what wonder was this? All at once the figures of Our Lady and her Child were no longer of marble, but of real flesh and blood!

When Mère Marie finally awoke, she was happier than she had ever been in her whole life. In that glorious dream Our Lady had bent down from her throne and had kissed her three times with unutterable tenderness! Never had she felt herself so much loved. Ah, did the heavenly one wish her to come to that strange land of rock and forest so that the people there might learn to know and love her Divine Son?

"I'm sure of it!" whispered Mère Marie excitedly. "But where is that vast country? And who was that young woman who traveled with me in the dream?"

When she had told the other Sisters about her experience, no one knew what to think. But some months later, when she confided the same matter to her Jesuit confessor, Père Jacques Dinet,* he had a partial solution. "I don't know who your companion was, Mother, but the country you dreamed about was probably Canada," he said thoughtfully. "And—well, maybe God wants you to go there as a missionary."

Mère Marie's heartbeat quickened. "Canada, Father! But where is that?"

Now it was Père Dinet's turn to be surprised. "Come, surely you've heard of Canada," he said, smiling. "Why, it's that great land across the Atlan-

---

*"Père" = French for "Father." ("Père" rhymes with "fair.")

tic where the Franciscans and the Jesuits have been
working for so many years! Indians live there,
Mother—men, women and children with red
skin—who know nothing of our holy Faith."

Mère Marie was alive with interest. "Tell me
more!" she pleaded.

So Père Dinet began to explain about the mysterious New World which lay across the ocean
nearly three thousand miles west of France. For
generations, he said, all Europe had believed that
China (rich in silks, perfumes and spices, perhaps
even in silver, gold and diamonds) could be reached
by sailing westward. Spain, England, Portugal, Hol-
land, France—all had sent explorers to try to find
such a passage to the Orient, although none had
been successful so far. However, on one of his many
westward journeys, a brave Frenchman named
Jacques Cartier had discovered the vast territory of
Canada. Indeed, just about a century before, on
August 10, 1535, he had sailed up a beautiful Canadian river which he had promptly named in honor
of the holy martyr Saint Lawrence, whose feast day
it was.

Mère Marie was all attention. "What has happened since, Father?"

The priest shrugged. "Not much. Since Canada
wasn't China, and since Cartier didn't bring home
any silks, spices or other wealth from there, the
King and his nobles weren't too interested in
spending money on further explorations. True, they
did allow Cartier to return to Canada several times,
but it was not until 1603 that our country became

really interested in the place. And then chiefly because of furs."

"Furs!"

"Yes, especially beaver furs, Mother, which are such a luxury here but which are worn even by children in the New World. Now, thanks to the efforts of another brave explorer, Samuel de Champlain, our country has sent scores of settlers to Canada, and we have a very profitable fur trade with the Indians."

"The settlers live in one place?"

"Yes, chiefly at Quebec, a little village which De Champlain founded on the banks of the Saint Lawrence in 1608. More than that. Good and honorable man that he is, De Champlain long ago saw to it that missionaries came to tell the Indians of the Faith. In 1615 he helped the Franciscans to establish themselves in Quebec. Ten years later he agreed that three Jesuit Fathers ought to join them: Enemond Massé, Charles Lalemant and Jean de Brébeuf."

"De Champlain is still living?"

"Yes, in Quebec. But he's sixty-eight years old now, Mother, and in very poor health."

When the interview was over, Mère Marie hurried to the chapel in a state of great excitement. If only Père Dinet were right! If only she could go to Canada, too! Surely the Jesuit missionaries, who had now replaced the Franciscans, needed help for their work among the Indians. Yet since she was a cloistered nun, with her present duties clearly marked out for her—

"Dear Lord, help me!" she prayed. "Let me want to do only what is Your will..."

But her prayer did not seem to be heard. Day succeeded day, and still Mère Marie was confused and anxious. Then one night, as she knelt in her cell, a mysterious Voice spoke in the depths of her soul:

"Ask Me by the Heart of Jesus, My most beloved Son. Through Him I will hear you and grant you your requests."

In a flash Mère Marie understood that the Sacred Heart of Jesus is the treasure house of every grace. "Father in Heaven, in the Name of the Sacred Heart of Jesus, tell me what You want of me," she whispered eagerly.

This prayer was answered some days later. As Mère Marie sat in her usual place in the chapel, she suddenly found herself once again in the land of her dream—the vast wilderness of mountain and forest, shrouded in mist. And as she gazed upon the awesome sight, the mysterious Voice spoke for the second time in the depths of her soul:

"This is Canada. You must go there and build a house for Jesus and Mary."

Mère Marie could scarcely contain her joy. Père Dinet had been right! She was to be a missionary to Canada! The wonderful dream of a few months back had been truly a sign from Heaven. What did it matter that for the moment her new vocation seemed an impossible one? In due course God would make clear His plans for her.

Although she tried to keep secret her new-found

interest in Canada, Mère Marie soon found herself
speaking so earnestly about the work of the Jesuit
missionaries there that all the nuns began to offer
prayers and sacrifices for them. In this regard, none
in the community was more enthusiastic than
nineteen-year-old Mère Marie de Saint Bernard.

"Those poor Jesuit priests in Canada are doing
very dangerous work, aren't they?" she asked Mère
Marie one day. "The pagan Indians are apt to kill
them."

Recalling what Père Dinet had had to say on this
very subject not so many days before, Mère Marie
nodded thoughtfully. "Yes, indeed, my dear. Any
priest who goes to Canada may become a martyr.
And not quickly either. Generally the Indians tor-
ture their victims for hours, or days, or longer."

The younger nun shuddered. "But that's just
because the poor creatures don't know any better,
Mother! Surely if someone had taught them about
God when they were little children, about love and
kindness and mercy—"

"They'd not do those terrible things?"

"No, I am sure they wouldn't. How much I'd like
to be able to help the Indians in Canada, especially
the children..."

Mère Marie hesitated. Little Mère Saint Bernard
was so slight and frail that at first the superiors had
felt convent life would be too much for her. Yet she
had persevered as a novice, and three years before
had taken her final vows. Now there was no more
cheerful or able worker in the whole community.

"My dear, all we can do for the little Indian

children right now is pray for them," she said consolingly. "God will bless our efforts, I know."

"Of course, Mother. Still, wouldn't it be nice if
the Jesuits in Canada would write to us about their
work there? About the food, the climate, the cus-
toms, the children?"

Mère Marie shook her head. "I'm afraid those
good men are far too busy for letter writing," she
said, smiling. "It must take all their time and
energy just to keep alive."

Some months later, however, Mère Marie realized
her error. In spite of their many labors in Canada,
the Jesuits were tireless letter writers. For years
they had been furnishing complete reports of their
missionary work to the superiors in France. These
Relations, as they were called, were so interesting
that a printer in Paris had agreed to set them up
in type and distribute copies all over the country.
Now Père Antoine Poncet of the Jesuit school in
Orléans (one of Claude's former teachers) had sent
Mère Marie a copy of the *Relation* for 1635.

Eagerly she read and reread the exciting story
of the missionary experiences of Père Paul Le
Jeune, superior of the Jesuits in Canada, and an
even more stirring account by Père Jean de
Brébeuf. Ah, what wonderful work these great men
were doing for God! And to think that Père Poncet
planned to join them! Even more. Had he not said
he was sure Mère Marie herself had a vocation to
work in Canada?

"It's almost as though he knew about the dream,"
she reflected, gazing at the two gifts which had

come with Père Poncet's letter: a miniature pilgrim's staff and a picture of Mère Anne de Saint Barthélemy, a heroic Spanish Carmelite nun who had left her own country to help establish her Order in France some years before.

A moment later, however, Mère Marie had ceased to dwell on the meaning of these little gifts. Once again she was reading that one sentence in Père Le Jeune's *Relation* which touched her to the quick: "Can there not be found a holy woman willing to gather the Blood of the Son of God for the salvation of the poor barbarians in these Canadian lands?"

"Oh, how willingly I'd be that woman if I could!" she sighed.

Yet even as her heart ached with longing, Mère Marie knew a deep sense of peace. What had the mysterious Voice told her only a few short months before? *"This is Canada. You must go there and build a house for Jesus and Mary."*

"Father in Heaven, whatever You wish," she said quietly.

But Mère Marie's good friend, Père Dinet, was less inclined to wait patiently upon the future. "The Jesuits need many nuns to help them in Canada," he told the Archbishop one day. "Already they've started classes for the Indian boys, but they think it only proper that teaching nuns should look after the girls."

Archbishop d'Eschaux, now in his middle eighties and severely crippled with rheumatism, jerked to painful attention. "Teaching nuns, Father! But you surely don't think I'd permit any nun in Tours to go to Canada?"

The priest shrugged. "Monseigneur, I'm thinking of just that."

"When the work there is so dangerous? So filled with hardship? No, no! I couldn't possibly agree."

Père Dinet took a deep breath, then he respectfully stated his case. "Monseigneur, the Jesuits report that unless the Indian girls—the future wives and mothers—are converted, the work among the boys will bear little fruit," he said. "Besides, shouldn't we try to help the many French families who have already gone to Canada as colonists? Since there are no teaching nuns in Quebec, how are their little daughters to be properly trained and educated? And the children of these children, when the time comes?"

The Archbishop's eyes grew thoughtful. "That is a problem," he admitted. "But—well, what can I do about it, Father?"

Père Dinet smiled. "I believe you yourself can start solving it right away, Monseigneur. After all, doesn't the answer lie right here in Tours?"

CHAPTER 3

THE TIME OF WAITING

SO WELL DID Père Dinet explain Mère Marie's great eagerness to work for souls in New France, as Canada was often called, that the Archbishop was impressed in spite of himself. When other priests also expressed their approval of the idea, he was finally won over completely. If Mother Prioress and her council were willing, he said, Mère Marie was free to go to Quebec whenever she wished. However, he could not finance the trip himself, or the building of a convent. For this some wealthy person must be found.

"What about such a benefactor?" he asked Père Dinet anxiously. "After all, with money so scarce these days—"

Père Dinet nodded happily. "Don't worry, Monseigneur. God will provide."

However, several months passed, and no wealthy person came forward to sponsor the cause of a girls' school in Canada. By the spring of 1637, Mère Françoise, the Prioress of the Ursulines, was almost certain that Mère Marie would spend the rest of her life in Tours. Therefore, she decided to appoint her to a new and responsible post.

"Mother, you've worked long enough with the novices," she declared one day. "From now on you'll be in charge of our boarding school."

But Mère Marie was far from showing disappointment. In fact, her dark eyes lit up with joy. "Mother, how can I thank you?" she burst out. "This is indeed good news!"

The Prioress stared in amazement. "But I was so afraid you'd be upset, my dear! After all those hopes of going to Canada—"

"I'm still going to Canada."

"*What?*"

"Yes, one of these days God will be sending the wealthy friend I've been asking of Him. In the meantime, how good to have some experience in teaching His little ones! Mother, how can I thank you for this favor?"

The Prioress shook her head in bewilderment. What childlike faith and trust! Truly, Mère Marie de l'Incarnation was a most remarkable woman. Yet was it really wise for her to continue to think of the missionary life? So far no nun in Europe had left her convent to labor in New France. And though Mère Marie's health was good, she was no longer exactly young. In fact, she would soon be thirty-eight years old.

"Don't worry about such things," said the Jesuits in Tours, when the Prioress' scruples were made known to them. "Mère Marie is one of God's chosen instruments."

The Jesuits in Paris and in Orléans were of like mind. "What we should be thinking of right now," they said, "is how Mère Marie's work in Canada is to be financed. After all, she can't start a girls' school without the help of some wealthy person."

Greatly consoled, Mother Prioress began to pray as fervently as anyone else that a benefactor would soon be found to help Mère Marie in her great work. But it was not until November 1638 that the many petitions were answered. Then the Prioress received a letter from one Madame Marie Madeleine de la Peltrie, a thirty-seven-year-old widow of Alençon. At the moment, this lady wrote, she was visiting the Jesuit house in Paris, where she had just made the acquaintance of Père Antoine Poncet. From him she had learned of Mère Marie and of her great interest in establishing a school for girls in the New World.

"May I help?" she asked in her letter. "Also, may I come to Tours to confer with Mère Marie?"

The Prioress was greatly reassured as she read a letter which had come in the same mail from Père Poncet himself. Madame de la Peltrie was a fine Christian woman, he declared. Her marriage had lasted but five short years, and her little daughter had died in infancy. Now not only was she alone, but she possessed a large fortune which she was willing to devote to the education of young girls in Canada.

"God be praised! It's what we've been praying for!" thought the Prioress, as she quickly went in search of Mère Marie.

Of course Mère Marie was overjoyed when she heard the news. True, it was a pity that for the time being Madame de la Peltrie's letter must be kept a secret. Certain of the lady's relatives, it seemed, were none too pleased that she wanted to spend her fortune on the children of New France. If they now discovered that she had asked for an Ursuline nun to accompany her to Quebec, they could make real trouble for the community.

Two months later, however, the situation had improved. Then Madame de la Peltrie wrote Mère Françoise that she might tell everything to her little family at the convent. "God willing, I'll come to see you in mid-February," she wrote.

Archbishop d'Eschaux, to whom Madame de la Peltrie had also confided her plans, was as excited as anyone else about the sudden turn of events. This charitable widow must be a wonderful Christian, he told Père Grand-Amy, the rector of the Jesuit college, when the latter dropped in at his house one morning for a brief visit. When she arrived in Tours surely she ought to be given the warmest of welcomes at the Ursuline convent, even permission to enter the cloister and to stay there for as long as she wished. In fact, he would be pleased if the nuns received Marie Madeleine de la Peltrie with all the honors they would show the Archbishop himself.

The rector chuckled. What a lovable old soul the Archbishop was! And how amusing that he seemed to have forgotten all his previous fears concerning Mère Marie's great ambition!

"Well, Monseigneur, I'll give Mother Prioress your message when I go to see her this afternoon," he said cheerfully. "And I suppose you'll want to meet Madame de la Peltrie yourself when she comes here next month?"

The Archbishop nodded eagerly. "Of course, Father, even before she visits the Ursulines. You'd best write her that today."

Soon Père Grand-Amy had dispatched his letter to Madame de la Peltrie. Mère Marie wrote, too— not once, but several times—for there were many details which she wished to discuss with this cherished new friend. Indeed, as the days passed, she had scarcely a moment to herself. Besides the letters she had to write there were her usual duties as directress of the boarding school and many talks with those nuns who had now decided that they also had a vocation to work in New France. Day after day, both young and old in the community came to beg Mère Marie for the privilege of going with her to Canada.

Mère Marie could scarcely find the words to answer them, since the choice of a co-worker did not actually rest with her. Only after much prayer and thought would the decision be made by the Prioress and her council. Nevertheless, her heart constantly went out to Mère Marie de Saint Bernard, the frail little nun who three years before had wished to hear more about the labors of the Jesuits in Quebec. Now twenty-two years old, she was still eager to go to Canada. In fact, she had recently promised Saint Joseph that she would ask her superior's permission to take his name for her own if he would help her get leave to go. Yes, she would be Marie de Saint Joseph, instead of Marie de Saint Bernard!

"I do love children so much," she told Mère Marie one day. "And I've the strangest notion that if I could just play on the viol for those little Indians—well, they'd love me, too, Mother. They'd want to hear all about God, Our Lady and the saints. My, we'd surely have the best time together, the little Indians and I . . ."

Mère Marie could not help smiling. "My dear, there's more to missionary work in Canada than just having a good time," she protested. "Think what the *Relations* tell us about the dreadful climate there—the ice and snow in winter, the heat in summer. Then, the food! Have you forgotten how the poor Jesuits often have nothing to eat but dried eels and a little corn meal? And not just for a day or so, but for weeks at a time?"

The younger nun shrugged. "I know, Mother. But who's to say that dried eels and corn meal aren't extremely nourishing? As for the weather—well, you know that many times we have ice and snow here in France. And great heat, too."

Such cheerful courage pleased Mère Marie. Secretly she admitted that it would be good to have this little nun as a co-worker in New France. Still, surely the superiors would never let her go because of her youth and frailty.

"My dear, let's leave everything in Saint Joseph's hands," she said finally. "After all, he does do wonders for those who trust in him."

During the next few weeks excitement mounted among the Ursulines in Tours. Madame de la Peltrie had promised to come to them in February. Now, what would she be like? And who among them besides Mère Marie would accompany her to New France?

Finally in mid-morning of February 19, young Pierre Duplette, still the Archbishop's trusted servant, appeared at the convent to announce that Madame de la Peltrie and her party had just arrived at the Jesuit college. In a few minutes, he said, Père Grand-Amy would escort them to the Archbishop's house. After partaking of some refreshments there, the group would leave for the convent.

"Is everything ready, Mother?" Pierre asked breathlessly of the Prioress. "Monseigneur is really anxious that Madame de la Peltrie be well received."

Mère Françoise nodded calmly. "Everything's ready, Pierre. We've rehearsed our little welcome several times. But tell me, have you yourself seen this lady?"

"Just for a moment," Pierre answered, "outside the Jesuit college. She seemed both charming and friendly, and much younger than thirty-seven years. However, there was an older gentleman with her who impressed me even more. Truly, this man had the face of a saint. He merely glanced at me, but in a flash I felt as though he had read my soul. I wonder who he is?"

The Prioress smiled. "That must have been Monsieur Jean de Bernières, Pierre—Madame de la Peltrie's friend and adviser. He is very much interested in the new convent in Canada."

"Monsieur de Bernières! But isn't he the royal treasurer at Caen? A man of great wealth and importance?"

"That's true. In this case, though, wealth and importance have not kept him from many good works. For instance, in Paris they say that Monsieur Vincent de Paul is happy to call Monsieur de Bernières his friend. In fact, some of the older nuns here are almost certain that we ought to let Monsieur de Bernières decide who shall be Mère Marie's companion to the New World. Indeed, they're almost as anxious to meet this holy man as they are to meet Madame de la Peltrie."

Pierre shrugged. "Well, they won't have much longer to wait. It's getting close to noon now. And by the way, Mother, our visitors are traveling very simply. Monsieur de Bernières has only two menservants in his carriage, Madame de la Peltrie but a single maid in hers."

Presently the Prioress and her community, as they filed into the courtyard to greet their guests at the convent gate, saw for themselves the truth of Pierre's report. Marie Madeleine de la Peltrie in a plain black dress, her blue eyes dancing with excitement, had all the grace and simplicity of a young girl. As for Jean de Bernières—his was the kindly smile and gentle courtesy of a true friend of God.

"Madame, Monsieur, a hundred thousand welcomes!" exclaimed Mère Françoise, hastening forward eagerly. "How good of you to come!"

Mère Marie's heartbeat quickened as she stood to one side with the other Sisters and watched the little scene. God be praised! Why, the youthful fair-haired Madame de la Peltrie was none other than the companion of her dream! The strange and beautiful dream of Canada five years ago...

Even as Mère Marie rejoiced, the strains of the *Veni Creator* suddenly filled the air. Now, as Archbishop d'Eschaux had requested, the community was preparing to escort the newcomers to the chapel with all the splendid ceremony generally reserved for him alone.

Creator Spirit, all divine,
Come visit every soul of Thine,
And fill with Thy celestial flame
The hearts which Thou Thyself didst frame...
Kindle with fire brought from above
Each sense, and fill our hearts with love;
And grant our flesh, so weak and frail,
The strength of Thine which ne'er may fail...

Madame de la Peltrie was amazed at the warmth and ceremony of her reception. But later that afternoon, as she and Mère Marie sat chatting in the convent parlor, she was even more impressed at what she heard.

"You mean you saw *me* in a dream?" she burst out eagerly. "But...but that's almost too much to believe, Mother!"

Mère Marie smiled. "Still, that's what happened,

Madame. It was you and no one else whom I took by the hand and almost dragged up the cliff to Our Lady's little church."

"I didn't want to come with you?"

"Oh, no! It was just that I was in such a hurry."

Madame de la Peltrie's blue eyes were alight. "Some years ago I, too, had a strange experience," she confessed. "Again it was a dream. Our Lord let me see Canada and all the poor Indians there. 'Will you go and help them?' He asked. Ah, Mère Marie, how unworthy I felt of such a great work! But Our Lord told me to be of good heart. The more unworthy a soul is, He said, the more He wishes to grant that soul great favors. 'I will use you as My tool,' He told me. 'In spite of many obstacles, you will go to Canada, and there you will end your days.'"

Mère Marie leaned forward eagerly. "Then what happened, Madame?"

"The vision of Canada slowly faded away, and I could hear Our Lord no longer. But a few weeks later—"

"Yes?"

"I fell gravely ill, and it seemed impossible that I would ever go to Canada. Still, with what strength I had I promised Saint Joseph to give myself and my fortune for God's work in New France if only he would ask Him to cure me."

"And the good Saint heard your prayer?"

"He did, Mother—and within just a few hours. My, how the doctors stared when they saw me up and around that very day!"

Mère Marie's heart beat fast. "Our Mère Marie

de Saint Bernard will surely want to hear this story," she said thoughtfully. "Poor dear, she, too, has long been praying to Saint Joseph for a great favor. May I tell her what you've just told me?"

Madame de la Peltrie nodded eagerly. "Of course, Mother. And say that I, too, will ask the good Saint to pray for her. The more prayers, the better, isn't that so?"

Wonder of wonders! When the community finally voted as to who should accompany Mère Marie to New France, the choice immediately fell upon the frail young Mère Marie de Saint Bernard. After each of the three ballots, her name had appeared to the exclusion of all others.

"My good Saint has worked a miracle, Mère Françoise!" the young nun told the Prioress, half laughing, half crying with joy. "How am I ever going to thank him? Then, Monsieur de Bernières..."

The Prioress was amused. "Come, child, what did he have to do with our vote?"

"Mother! You know that Madame de la Peltrie asked Monsieur de Bernières to interview everyone who wished to go to Canada. I do believe that after I had spoken to him in the parlor, he put in a good word for me with the rest of the community. Now, isn't that so?"

"Well—"

"Dear Mother, you know it is! And to think I was so timid about telling him of my hopes! And Madame de la Peltrie, too! Why, Mère Marie almost had to drag me to see them in the parlor..."

The Prioress smiled. "Look, my dear, there's no need to worry," she said soothingly. "For a long time now Monsieur de Bernières has had the reputation of being one who can read souls. If he said you can help Mère Marie and Madame de la Peltrie do their work in Canada, it surely must·be so. And by the way, the community hasn't forgotten your promise to Saint Joseph. They want you to have his name for your own from now on."

The young Ursuline scarcely knew what to say. What truly blessed news this day had brought! Yet even as she struggled to express her gratitude, the Prioress shook her head.

"Now, dear, you'd best go and pack your things instead of trying to make a speech," she urged. "Or have you forgotten that your companions expect to leave within thirty-six hours?"

Thirty-six hours! Quickly Mère Saint Joseph brushed back her tears of joy. "I had forgotten!" she burst out excitedly. "Oh, how can I be ready in such a short time?"

At the end of the day all was in order, save for the fact that Madame de la Peltrie's maid suddenly decided she had neither the courage nor the desire to live in Canada. In spite of this excitement, things were arranged in time for the departure ceremony on the morning of February 22. Mère Marie and Mère Saint Joseph, having heard Mass at the Archbishop's house and received his blessing, were in the convent courtyard embracing their Ursuline sisters for the last time. Nearly everyone was weeping save the missionaries themselves and Charlotte

THE LONG JOURNEY TO CANADA
WAS ABOUT TO BEGIN.

Barré, a native of Tours, who was taking the place of the timid maid. Her confessor had heard of the sudden withdrawal of Madame de la Peltrie's maid and had suggested this fine young girl as a substitute.

"What, Charlotte! No tears?" asked Jean de Bernières jovially, as they stood watching the touching scene.

The girl's face was radiant. "Of course not, Monsieur! Why should I cry when this is such a happy day for me?"

"You really want to go to New France?"

"I most certainly do."

"You won't be afraid of the hardships, as was Madame de la Peltrie's former maid?"

"Oh, no! I have a great desire to see Canada."

"But you're so young, child! Only eighteen!"

"I'll be nineteen next month, Monsieur, and I do love to travel."

"Well, Charlotte, I think you'll be a great help to all my good friends," Jean de Bernières said after a thoughtful pause. "Just remember, though, that it's a long, long way to Canada. Even with the best of luck you won't reach our colony at Quebec before midsummer."

The girl nodded. "I know, Monsieur. I understand that before we go, Madame de la Peltrie and Mère Marie must spend much time in Orléans and Paris, talking to many important people."

"That's right. But there's something else you ought to know, Charlotte. Mère Marie may have serious trouble when she reaches Orléans. If it comes, do try to console her all you can."

Charlotte's eyes widened. "Trouble in Orléans, Monsieur! But why?"

Smiling, Jean de Bernières shook his head and motioned toward the gate. At last the farewells were over. To the joyful pealing of the bells in the convent tower, the little group of missionaries was now passing from the cloistered courtyard into the street.

"Come along to your carriage, child," he said kindly. "I'll explain to you later what I mean."

CHAPTER 4

IN ORLÉANS

ON THE seventy-mile journey to Orléans, it
was Mère Saint Joseph who explained to
Charlotte the reason for their anxiety.
Madame Claude Buisson, it seemed, was very dis-
pleased that her sister wanted to spend the rest of
her life caring for the children of New France. The
work was far beneath her, she had said, as well as
extremely dangerous.

"So Madame Buisson has tried her best to keep
Mère Marie from leaving Tours, even threatening
the Archbishop with a lawsuit for his part in the
affair," Mère Saint Joseph ended.

"It isn't possible!" Charlotte exclaimed as she
listened.

"Oh, yes! She got nowhere with such tactics,
though. Or with the Mayor either, when she tried
them on him. Then just a few days ago Madame
Buisson came to the convent parlor accompanied
by her lawyer. She was angrier than ever. Believe
it or not, she then and there cut off young Claude's
allowance—the money from the Buisson estate that

has been used to feed and clothe the boy, and keep
him in school since his mother joined the Ursulines
eight years ago."

"Now the lad is penniless?"

"Quite penniless."

"Dear God! What's to become of him?"

"Who can say? But we are all sure there'll be a
dreadful scene when Mère Marie finally goes to the
Jesuit school in Orléans and tells him of what's
happened."

"The Jesuit school in Orléans! Is that where
Claude is now?"

"Yes, he's been studying there for quite some
time. To make matters worse, Charlotte, the boy
hasn't the slightest notion that his mother is leaving
for Canada, and that he'll probably never see her
again. Long ago Mère Marie decided that it would
be kinder to break the news in person, rather than
by letter. But now that his aunt has cut him off
without a penny—well, do you begin to understand
why Monsieur de Bernières is so worried? Why he
has asked you to console Mère Marie as best you
can when the time comes?"

Tears filled Charlotte's eyes. So it was indeed true
that trouble awaited poor Mère Marie in Orléans!
"Of course!" she exclaimed. "I'll do everything possible to help her, Mother."

As the carriages proceeded at a brisk pace along
the rough and dusty road to Orléans, no one spoke
openly of Mère Marie's problem. Still, she herself
sensed the sympathy of her companions and was
grateful for it. As soon as possible after reaching

Orléans, she reflected, she would seek out the nearest church and pray for light and strength to make her boy understand what God was asking of him.

However, it was only a few minutes after the travelers had arrived at the inn in Orléans, where Jean de Bernières had reserved quarters for them, that nineteen-year-old Claude Martin casually appeared at the front entrance. Mère Marie, preparing to leave for church, could scarcely believe her eyes.

"Claude! My boy!"

A slight smile brightened the youth's face, but he made no attempt to embrace his mother. "My, what a surprise, Maman!" he exclaimed, bowing politely. "Don't tell me that you've run away from the Ursulines!"

Mère Marie started back as though she had been struck. The little jest was so out of place! Then, the odd coolness in Claude's voice, the aloofness in his eyes—

"Darling, something's wrong!" she burst out. "You're ill, or else things have gone wrong at school. What is it? Tell me!"

Still smiling his peculiar smile, Claude shook his head. "Oh, no, Maman," he said easily. "Nothing's wrong. I was merely wondering what brings you out of your cloister. Or is that a question you don't want to answer?"

"Of course I'll answer, Claude! I've come to Orléans on. . .well, on business."

"Business! And when this business is finished?"

"Then I go to Paris."

"And after that?"

"Well, I . . . I go to Dieppe."

"And then, Maman, perhaps you go still farther away? Much, much farther away?"

A sudden fear clutched at Mère Marie's heart as Claude drew from his pocket that dreadful document, so recently signed in the convent parlor, by which he had been cut off from the Buisson estate without a single penny.

"Surprised, Maman? This was delivered to me only a few minutes ago by the very coachman who brought you here."

Mère Marie could scarcely believe her ears. In one last effort to keep her from leaving, her own sister had tricked an innocent man into setting Claude against her.

"My son—"

"There's a letter here from Aunt Claude, too, Maman, telling all about your plans for the future. Apparently she thinks you care more for the little Indians in Canada than you do for me."

"Darling, if you'll just listen for a moment—"

Suddenly Claude stiffened, while his voice blazed with indignation. "Listen!" he burst out. "Why should I listen to someone who's never really loved me? Eight years ago, Maman, you went away to become a nun. That was bad enough. Now, though, to go thousands of miles across the ocean, to leave me without a home or money, to keep everything a secret until the last minute—how could you do it?"

"CLAUDE, HAVE YOU EVER WANTED FOR ANYTHING
SINCE I LEFT YOU EIGHT YEARS AGO?"

Mère Marie lowered her eyes. Dear God, how the devil wanted to keep her from saving souls in New France! To what lengths he would go, even to setting her own dear ones against her! Yet Heaven must always prevail against Hell...always... always...

"Claude," she said, her voice suddenly firm and steady, "have you ever wanted for anything since I left you eight years ago?"

"W-what?"

"You heard me, dear. Have you ever needed food, clothes, shelter, friends, since you were eleven years old?"

Biting his lip, Claude turned abruptly away. "I...I'm going now, Maman. I don't want to talk about things any more."

Quickly Mère Marie reached out for her boy's hand. "Darling, you didn't answer me," she said gently. "Are you really afraid to be honest? Do you really think God won't give you everything you need in the future?"

As he glanced briefly into his mother's dark eyes, so full of love and tenderness, the youth's bitterness melted away in spite of himself. "I...I shouldn't have spoken as I did, Maman," he muttered. "Please forgive me! Truly, though, to learn of your plans like this—"

Mère Marie nodded. "I understand, darling. It was a cruel shock. Still, perhaps this was really the best way for both of us."

"The best way!"

"Yes, son. For we both suffered, didn't we? Now,

if we cheerfully offer the suffering to God, who is All-Just, He will bless us with graces that we didn't merit a few minutes ago. Ah, what a pity that people so often try to run away from God's will, when that will is always right for them!"

For a moment Claude was silent. What faith his mother had! What courage and selflessness!

"Maman, in the past I've not thought too much about God's will," he finally admitted in a choked voice. "I . . . I've only been interested in my own. But—well, perhaps things could be different from now on."

Mère Marie was startled. What wonder was this? "Different, dear? How different?"

"I . . . I don't know, Maman. But if I burn this wretched document that Aunt Claude sent me—"

"Oh, my son!"

"If I write her that I don't want the Buisson money, and that I thoroughly approve of your going to Canada—"

Mère Marie stared in amazement. What was the boy trying to tell her? "Look, darling, God wants us to love Him . . ." she began soothingly. "Of course, if you really want to make this sacrifice for Him . . ."

Little by little Claude's face brightened. "Then I'll do it," he said resolutely. "I'll do it right away. Maybe afterward God will give me one grace that I've never dared to ask of Him."

"One grace?"

"That's right. But don't try to find out what it is, Maman. I'm not ready to talk about it yet."

Puzzled though she was by this statement, Mère Marie knew great peace as she and Claude presently entered the parish church together. God be praised! At last the much-dreaded trouble in Orléans was over and done with...

The next day, though, as she and her companions set out on the second lap of their journey, Mère Marie's heart was close to breaking. She had just said good-bye to Claude! Probably never again, at least in this world, would she see him or hear his voice.

"Poor soul!" whispered Charlotte Barré to Madame de la Peltrie as their carriage rolled swiftly through the drab February countryside en route to Paris. "This must be like martyrdom for Mère Marie. Can't we do something to help her, Madame? After all, Monsieur de Bernières did tell me—"

Madame de la Peltrie smiled and shrugged. "No, my dear, we'll not try to console Mère Marie just now. Early this morning she told me that we mustn't try to make things easy for her after she had said good-bye to Claude and that during the journey she wished to pray for his special intention."

Charlotte's eyes widened. "His special intention! Have you any idea what that can be?"

"Not yet. But perhaps we'll find out in Paris."

This proved to be true. Shortly after their arrival in the great city, while Madame de la Peltrie and Mère Marie were busily arranging for their approaching sea voyage to the New World, there came extraordinary news from Orléans. Claude Martin, it seemed, had decided to become a Jesuit priest. Even now he was on his way to Paris for an interview with the superiors.

Mère Saint Joseph could scarcely contain her joy. "Why, it's the answer to all our prayers!" she told Jean de Bernières. "Don't you agree, Monsieur?"

The latter's eyes narrowed. "No, Mother," he said abruptly, "I don't agree at all."

"But, Monsieur! If Claude is to study for the priesthood in the Society of Jesus, that means Mère Marie can go to Canada without having to worry about his future."

"True."

"Surely this was the lad's special intention that we've all been praying for! But why aren't you happy about the good news?"

Jean de Bernières shook his head regretfully. "Because," he said, "I don't feel the time to rejoice has come."

"What?"

"Somehow I feel that Mère Marie's work in Canada will succeed only at the price of great suffering, much of which will be caused by her boy."

"But—"

"Mark my words, Mère Saint Joseph. The Jesuits won't accept Claude Martin for the priesthood— now, or at any other time."

CHAPTER 5

THE JOURNEY

JEAN DE BERNIÈRES was right. Claude's sudden willingness to study for the priesthood in the Society of Jesus might be considered a near miracle by his mother and his friends, but not by the Jesuits in Paris. Steadfastly the Provincial refused to accept the boy as a candidate. It would be much better, he said, for him to continue his regular schooling in Orléans.

Early in April, when it was almost time to leave for Dieppe, the travelers had still another disappointment. Suddenly the Archbishop of Paris reversed his earlier decision that Mère Catherine de Saint Jérôme, a local Ursuline, might go with Mère Marie to Canada. Now, he said, she must unpack her things at once. It was too dangerous for a woman to be a missionary in New France.

"What troubles we're having!" said Charlotte Barré to Madame de la Peltrie as they finally set out on the one-hundred-mile journey to the seaport town of Dieppe. "Truly, Madame, I'm beginning to wonder—"

"What, Charlotte?"

"If we'll ever have any good luck at all!"

The instant laughter of Madame de la Peltrie was like the sound of silver bells. "Why, of course we'll have good luck, my dear! In just a little while we'll be on the high seas, in a fine boat named in honor of Saint Joseph. Doesn't that give you confidence?"

The girl's eyes brightened. "Oh, yes, Madame! Saint Joseph will take care of us, I know. Still, it would have been so much nicer—"

"If Claude's future could have been settled?"

"That's it. If only Mère Marie could leave France knowing that her boy had a home, with someone to help him with his problems! But this way—well, it's heartbreaking, Madame, that's what it is. Truly heartbreaking!"

Madame de la Peltrie nodded. "I agree with you," she said thoughtfully. "But of course Monsieur de Bernières is a wealthy man, and will do what he can for Claude. Besides, remember what Mère Marie keeps telling us, and Monsieur de Bernières, too. The success of the work in Canada depends chiefly on our faith in God—real faith—no matter what happens. So I've decided I won't worry any more, not even about Claude. Ah, my dear, if you could just try to do the same!"

Such a plea had the desired effect, and soon Charlotte was her usual cheerful self. By the time the carriages had reached Dieppe, the other travelers were feeling happier, too, especially when they gazed for the first time at the shining expanse of ocean below the town and saw the *Saint Joseph,* their boat, riding at anchor in the outer harbor. Truly, the difficulties of the past now seemed much less important.

It was good, too, to meet the other nuns and priests who would be traveling with them to New France: Mère Cécile de Saint Croix, an Ursuline from Dieppe; Père Barthélemy Vimont, the newly appointed superior of the Jesuit missions in Canada; and three Augustinian nuns who were to open the first hospital there—Mères Marie de Saint Ignace, Anne de Saint Bernard and Marie de Saint Bonaventure. Also, four more Jesuit Fathers were about to take passage on another vessel, including Antoine Poncet, Pierre Chaumonont, Nicolas Gondoin and a lay brother, Claude Yager.

"Three Ursulines, three Augustinians, five Jesuits and two laywomen," mused Jean de Bernières happily. "Why, that makes thirteen people, Mère Marie—a real family of pioneers!"

The latter's eyes shone. "That's right, Monsieur. A pity, though, that this same family can't be fourteen."

"Fourteen?"

"Ah, Monsieur, if only you were coming with us!"

Jean de Bernières chuckled. "I think God prefers that I remain in France, Mother, to help your work in other ways. After all, though many have promised to remember you with prayers and money, in time their memories may prove to be disappointingly weak. Then a letter or a visit from me should be quite useful, don't you agree?"

Mère Marie was overcome with gratitude. What

a good friend their little group had in Jean de Bernières!

"May the Lord bless you, Monsieur," she said earnestly. "Certainly we shall never forget you in our prayers."

Although the missionaries would have preferred to leave Dieppe at once, it was several weeks before Captain Bontemps of the *Saint Joseph* decided that wind and weather were favorable enough to set sail. Finally, on the morning of May 4, came the exciting hour of departure.

"Father in Heaven, please bless the work we're going to try to do for You in Canada," whispered Mère Marie, as she stood dry-eyed on deck and gazed at her beloved homeland for the last time. "Let us help save many souls. Bless my boy, too. . . ."

Standing a few feet away, little Mère Saint Joseph waved gaily at the fast-receding coastline of France. What a relief to be putting out to sea! Only a few days before her parents had almost succeeded in keeping her at home. Even her beloved uncle, the Bishop of La Rochelle, had decided that the work in Quebec would be too hard for her, and that she ought to return to Tours. At the last minute, however, Dom Raymond, Mère Marie's former confessor, had succeeded in setting everyone's mind at ease. Now, God be praised, all the trouble was over.

For a few days it did seem as though Mère Saint Joseph were right. Not only were her difficulties at an end, but those of her companions as well. The weather was fair, the sea was as smooth as glass, and their quarters were spacious and comfortable.

Each morning Père Vimont came to offer the Holy Sacrifice of the Mass and to preach an inspiring sermon. At various other times the Augustinian and the Ursuline nuns recited the Little Office of the Blessed Virgin together.

"It's just as though we were back in France in our own convent chapel," they told one another happily.

Mère Cécile, who had volunteered to leave her Ursuline community in Dieppe in order to help in the founding of the first girls' school in Canada, was vastly relieved that the journey was proving so uneventful.

"Not a pirate ship in sight!" she told Captain Bontemps one sunshiny morning. "Isn't that wonderful, Captain?"

The captain chuckled. "Now, Mother! Did you really expect that kind of excitement?"

Mère Cécile smiled and shrugged. France and England had been having political difficulties for years, and the Atlantic was known to be infested with ruthless English pirates who were bent on capturing whatever French vessels they could. Of course the other nuns also understood this, but they had lived in the interior of the country. Never had they heard the harrowing tales told by the fishermen of Dieppe who had barely escaped with their lives after a savage pirate attack.

"Well, I suppose I was prepared for the worst," admitted Mère Cécile. "Now, though, it's hard to imagine that anything could spoil the peace of this enormous and beautiful ocean. Why, just look,

Captain! Have you ever seen anything more glorious?"

Captain Bontemps smiled briefly as Mère Cécile pointed beyond the prow of the ship. The waters of the Atlantic, rippled by a gentle breeze from the south, stretched for endless miles under the warm May sun in a glitter of brilliant greens and deep blues. Occasionally a small wave broke into a plume of white foam, then lost itself in a whirlpool of glistening bubbles.

"Yes, Mother, the sea is beautiful today," he conceded, "the air clean and fresh. Nevertheless, we're quite prepared for what may happen later on."

"Bad weather?"

An anxious look crossed Captain Bontemps' grizzled features. "That's it. We do expect a bit of a storm."

Mère Cécile's blue eyes clouded with disbelief. "On such a glorious day as this?" she burst out. "But...but that's impossible!"

"Not at all, Mother," the Captain said. "To the north we still have the cold winds of winter; to the south, the warm winds of spring. Tonight, perhaps, when the two winds meet on either side of us—ah, maybe then you'll be wishing that the pirates had captured us, and that we were safe on land, even in an English prison!"

The captain's concern with the weather proved to be well founded. By late afternoon a chill wind from the north had piled ominous black clouds high in the sky and turned the peaceful Atlantic into a turbulent mass of mountainous gray waves.

Huddled in their cabin, the nuns tried to be calm. But as darkness fell and the _Saint Joseph_ began to roll helplessly from side to side, groaning and creaking in every timber, one after another of them grew tense with fear. Dear God, what was going to happen next?

"Lightning!" cried Madame de la Peltrie suddenly, as an enormous sheet of flame swept through the inky blackness outside, to be followed by a clap of thunder that seemed to split the world. "We've been struck by lightning!"

Mère Cécile covered her eyes. "Holy Mother!" she groaned. "Now we'll never see Canada! We'll go to our deaths out here in the middle of nowhere. . . ."

Pale-faced and trembling, for she had not been feeling well even before the storm, Mère Marie clutched her rosary. "No, no!" she gasped. "Let's ask Our Lady to help us! Isn't she the Star of the Sea?" And quickly the terrified little group began to offer the familiar and consoling prayer of the Rosary.

In spite of their fervent prayers, however, the storm continued to rage. Even when the worst was over, Père Vimont was unable to offer Holy Mass for thirteen days because of the extremely high seas. Yet the sturdily built _Saint Joseph_ managed to ride out the rough weather.

Finally the skies cleared and Captain Bontemps announced that there was no longer need for anyone to be afraid of shipwreck. True, their vessel had been blown many miles to the north of her course, but with the present favorable wind she would soon make up for lost time.

"This surely calls for a celebration," he told Madame de la Peltrie that afternoon as she emerged from her quarters, pale and woebegone after the recent ordeal. "Don't you agree, Madame? Perhaps a specially good dinner tonight for you and your companions, with fireworks afterward?"

Shuddering, Madame de la Peltrie turned her head. "Dinner? Thank you, no!"

"But, my dear lady—"

"None of us could eat a bite. We. . .we died a thousand deaths during the storm."

"But the storm is over, Madame! Now you and the good nuns must build up your strength for all the work that lies ahead."

"The good nuns are in their beds, Captain. They have no wish to leave them."

"Well, they must leave them, Madame. At once! Fresh air, nourishing food, mild exercise—there's no better cure for seasickness than a combination of these three. Besides," and the Captain's eyes began to twinkle, "I've just thought of something. Tell them that tonight's celebration will be in honor of Our Lady and Saint Joseph, who surely saved us from death during the storm. Would they be so ungrateful as to stay away?"

For a moment Marie Madeleine de la Peltrie was silent. Then she took a deep breath. "Well, when you put it like that—"

"Good, Madame! Very good! I knew you'd understand. Now, will you go at once to Mère Marie and her companions and try to get them to understand, too?"

In spite of herself, Madame de la Peltrie managed a faint smile. What a persistent man the Captain was! "All right, I'll go," she said. "But the poor nuns and Charlotte are really as weak as little rabbits, Captain. I can promise nothing. Nothing at all."

Wonder of wonders! The Captain's ailing passengers did agree to try his prescription of fresh air, good food and mild exercise. They found it to be most effective. Indeed, by the time the evening's celebration was over, everyone was feeling much better.

"I didn't think I could enjoy a dinner so much," Madame de la Peltrie told Charlotte, as they walked briefly on deck before retiring for the night. "And the fireworks! Weren't they splendid?"

The girl nodded eagerly. "Indeed they were, Madame. I never saw such glorious stars and rockets—red, green, silver, blue, gold—a host of colors! Still, I can't help wondering why we happened to have fireworks on board. Do the people in Canada really need such luxuries from France?"

Madame de la Peltrie's eyes twinkled. "Of course. The Jesuits always like to have a fireworks display for their Indian converts on special feastdays. They say it helps to impress upon them something of the glory of God and His saints. In fact, it's quite possible that there'll be such a celebration for us when we reach Quebec. After all, remember we're bringing to the colonists the good news of the birth of the little prince last September?"

"That's right. Our future King Louis XIV—God bless him!"

An hour or so later, as she settled herself for sleep, Charlotte's thoughts turned briefly to the hundreds of letters and packages which the *Saint Joseph* was now carrying in her hold. My, how important these were! For not only did the people in Quebec know nothing of the birth of little Prince Louis nearly a year before, but in all that time they had not received any other news from France, or supplies either. And why? Because ships could sail for Canada only from late March through June. If they left before or after these times, they would find much of the ocean and the Saint Lawrence River blocked with treacherous ice.

"Dear Lord, please let us reach Quebec in safety," whispered Charlotte sleepily. "The people there must need so many things. . . ."

For the next few days the *Saint Joseph* pushed steadily westward under full sail and clear skies. But one day in mid-June, early on Trinity Sunday, a dense fog rolled in from the north, and the helmsman was ordered to proceed with extreme caution.

Captain Bontemps told Père Vimont, as they walked on deck together, that he feared not only that they might collide with another vessel, but worse: they were still so far north because of the storm that they could easily meet an iceberg.

Père Vimont shuddered. "An iceberg? God forbid! Why, we might be smashed to bits!"

"Exactly. Yet it happens all the time, Father. My

cousin Jacques—Lord rest his soul—went to his death in just that fashion three years ago. And his whole ship with him."

Suddenly the priest's eyes brightened. "But look, Captain! Isn't the fog beginning to lift over there?"

Captain Bontemps stared, then shook his head. "Only a trifle, Father. We must pray for much more hopeful signs."

The day continued cold and overcast. Then late in the afternoon, when the nuns had finished chanting Vespers in their cabin, the alarm sounded. A huge iceberg had just been sighted through the fog! Worse still, it was headed directly toward the ship!

"Holy Virgin, what'll we do?" cried Mère Cécile, rushing frantically on deck with Mère Saint Joseph. "We'll be crushed to death!"

Following close behind, Mère Marie urged her two friends to be calm. Yet as she, too, saw the ghastly hulk of green-blue ice now bearing down upon them, her heart sickened. How could the water support such a stupendous weight? Why, the iceberg was like a castle, a floating city, its towering summit entirely hidden in the fog. . . .

"It can't be real!" she whispered. "It's a terrible dream!"

But a moment later, as a scream went up from the passengers and crew now assembled on deck, Mère Marie knew full well that she was not dreaming. Somehow the helmsman, confused and panic-stricken, had just turned his wheel in the wrong direction. Now the *Saint Joseph* was scarcely a hundred yards from the cruel mountain of ice.

"Father in Heaven, the poor wretch has done for us all!" groaned Captain Bontemps, falling on his knees. "It's the end of everything!"

Père Vimont still had hope, however. Having given general absolution to the passengers and crew, he now made a hurried vow to the Blessed Virgin. If she would save the ship, he promised, all present would make a vow to serve her for the rest of their days.

"Y-yes, that's w-what we'll d-do!" gasped a young sailor, who was scarcely more than a boy.

Now little Mère Saint Joseph, remarkably calm and self-possessed, began to move among the crowd and urge them to recite the Litany of Loreto.

At once a trembling chorus of men's and women's voices rose to Heaven:

> *Holy Mary, pray for us!*
> *Holy Mother of God, pray for us!*
> *Holy Virgin of Virgins, pray for us!*

Even as she joined in the familiar words, Mère Marie's heartbeat quickened. Could it be that the *Saint Joseph*, now less than two hundred feet from the swiftly moving iceberg, was turning slightly aside? That the helmsman, in one last desperate effort—

"A miracle, Mother!" cried Captain Bontemps excitedly, as he, too, sensed what was happening. "Look!"

Unable to speak now, or even to pray, Mère Marie stood rooted to the spot. The monstrous iceberg, hissing like a deadly serpent, had just slipped by

THE MONSTROUS ICEBERG
WAS ALMOST UPON THE *SAINT JOSEPH*.

the *Saint Joseph,* missing her by inches! In a minute, two minutes at the most, it would be swallowed up in the fog!

"A miracle!" echoed the passengers and crew, as they also realized their great good fortune.

"God be praised!"

As she stood watching the joyful confusion, Mère Marie found herself weeping like a lost child who has finally come home. Actually she had been willing to drown in the icy waters of the Atlantic, if God also had been willing. But He had not. Instead, it now seemed to her that from all eternity He had planned that she should tell the little ones of Canada about Himself. Soon, perhaps in one short month, the great work would begin.

But it was not until July 21 that the missionaries finally set foot on Canadian soil. This was at Tadoussac, a trading post on the Saint Lawrence River, one hundred and fifty miles east of Quebec. Here, since the *Saint Joseph* would be unloading cargo for several days, the nuns decided to transfer to the *Saint Jacques*—a smaller boat that was about ready to sail for Quebec with a load of codfish.

"Well, Mothers, we've an hour or so to spare," their new captain told the nuns good-naturedly. "How would you like to go ashore and see some Indians? I'd be glad to act as a guide."

They looked at one another eagerly. "Could you really do that, Captain?" asked Mère Marie. "We've never seen an Indian."

The Captain laughed. "That makes a nice balance, Mother. The Indians have never seen a nun.

This way, now—and watch your step!"

Soon everyone was enjoying a wonderful new experience. More than fifty Indians lived in Tadoussac—men, women and children with shining red-bronze skin, straight black hair and solemn dark eyes. Though they were ragged and poor and their wigwams incredibly dirty, they greeted the nuns respectfully. Indeed, in just a short time all the children—clad in little more than scraps of deerskin, and round-eyed with wonder—had gathered about the newcomers to see and touch their habits and rosaries.

"Goodness, this poor baby can't understand a word I'm saying!" laughed Mère Saint Joseph, hugging one little girl to herself. "Look, Mère Marie, isn't she beautiful?"

"Oh, look at this little darling!" exclaimed Madame de la Peltrie, picking up a solemn-faced three-year-old and kissing her warmly. "See, she's not a bit afraid."

Mère Marie's face was radiant. In spite of their rags and dirt, the Indians of Tadoussac were wonderfully appealing. Yet—well, what was that terrible odor?

"Just bear grease, Mother," laughed the Captain, reading her thoughts. "All the Indians rub themselves with it, or something similar, to make their skin shine. Then you'd better learn right now that these poor people never wash. And that every last one of them has fleas."

"Fleas!"

"That's right, Mother. And lice, too."

Still holding their new little friends, Mère Saint Joseph and Madame de la Peltrie looked at each other in sudden dismay. Then they burst out laughing. Mère Marie laughed, too. There was going to be plenty of work to do in Canada...

Charlotte Barré joined in the general merriment. "What kind of Indians are these?" she asked the Captain eagerly. "Iroquois, perhaps?"

The captain shook his head. "No, Mademoiselle. They're Montagnais, of the Algonquin tribe. The Iroquois, thank God, are several miles to the south of us, across the Saint Lawrence River. And they are not one nation, as some suppose, but five distinct groups: Mohawks, Oneidas, Onondagas, Cayugas and Senecas."

Madame de la Peltrie looked shrewdly at the Captain. "Something tells me that you don't love the Iroquois," she said with mock severity. "Why not, when God made them to be our brothers?"

The Captain's eyes twinkled. "When you've been here a bit longer, Madame, you yourself may find it hard to love these fiends out of Hell."

"Good Heavens! Are they as bad as that?"

"Bad? The Iroquois are troublemakers of the worst sort, Madame, in league with the English to run us out of Canada. But I don't think you'll be bothered by them at Quebec. The place has been too well fortified by our Governor, Charles de Montmagny."

Mère Marie was thoughtful. "Monsieur de Montmagny is the successor of the good Samuel de Champlain, isn't he?"

The Captain nodded. "He is that, Mother, and a most worthy successor, too. The good Samuel de Champlain died four years ago this coming Christmas Day in the arms of Père Charles Lalemant."

"You knew de Champlain, Captain?"

Mère Marie thought of the wonderful things she had heard about Samuel de Champlain and his efforts to bring over missionary priests.

"I did, Mother, and a better man never lived. Canada's well-being was his love, his life. Ah, may God help Monsieur de Montmagny to continue in his footsteps! So far, he's been doing very well indeed."

CHAPTER 6

ARRIVAL AT QUEBEC

WHEN THEY finally returned to the *Saint Jacques*, Mère Marie and her companions made a startling discovery. Owing to the lack of cargo space, a large quantity of evil-smelling codfish had been stacked to the ceiling of their tiny cabin. Now only a few square feet of floor remained clear.

"Good heavens, someone's made a terrible mistake!" declared Madame de la Peltrie indignantly. "How are eight of us going to sleep in here? We'd better speak to the Captain at once."

Mère Marie shook her head. "No, let's not bother him," she pleaded. "After all, this is a fishing boat. The Captain didn't have to take us on as passengers, especially when we gave him so little notice."

"That's right," put in Mère Cécile quickly. "Besides, we ought to be grateful that we have all this fish to take to Quebec. Certainly the people there will find use for it."

"All I can think of right now is that we're not wasting any time by sailing on the *Saint Jacques*,"

Charlotte broke in cheerfully. "We'll reach Quebec far sooner than if we'd waited in Tadoussac for the *Saint Joseph* to make the trip."

Madame de la Peltrie smiled and shrugged. "Well, that's true enough," she admitted. "I guess we won't bother the Captain after all."

During the next few days, however, as the *Saint Jacques* pushed steadily up the Saint Lawrence on the one-hundred-and-fifty-mile journey to Quebec, even Mère Marie was forced to admit that living conditions on the little vessel were deplorable. What heat from the July sun! What odor from the codfish! But there was a great consolation aboard the *Saint Jacques*—the chance to hear three more Masses each day. For at Tadoussac, Père Vimont had been joined by Pères Poncet, Chaumonont and Gondoin, who had already made a successful crossing from Dieppe. Every morning on deck, using a crude packing case for an altar, each of the four priests offered the Holy Sacrifice for the success of their own work, as well as for that of the Ursulines and their Augustinian companions.

Very soon, however, the missionaries experienced new hardships. Though the July heat continued unabated, it was now accompanied by heavy showers. Shoes, clothes, bedding—all were damp, moldy and strong with the odor of codfish. Nothing would dry. In fact, on July 31, when the *Saint Jacques* put in for the night at the Ile d'Orléans, an uninhabited island some seven miles below Quebec, young Charlotte Barré was almost in tears. In the morning, she was thinking, they would arrive at Quebec. Then, according to the Captain, the Governor and his officials would have a fine reception for them. Yet how could Madame de la Peltrie appear before these notables in miserably dirty clothes that reeked of codfish? As for the poor nuns in their all-but-ruined habits—

"My dear, we won't worry about anything," said Madame de la Peltrie cheerfully. "After all, we've had a long, hard trip of three months. The good people of Quebec won't expect too much of us."

Charlotte swallowed hard. "But you engaged me to be your maid, Madame! To take care of your clothes, to keep them clean and nice! Yet what have I done during these last ten days on the *Saint Jacques?* Nothing! Absolutely nothing, because of all the heat and the mold and the terrible rains! I've failed you miserably, Madame, and I'm so ashamed. . . ."

That night, though, when camp had been made in some deserted wigwams on the Ile d'Orléans, Mère Marie quickly set Charlotte's mind at ease.

"Let's offer up to God whatever embarrassment we have tomorrow for the success of our work in Canada," she suggested. "And please don't feel that you've failed Madame de la Peltrie in any way. You've really been a marvelous comfort to her since we left Tours."

Greatly consoled, Charlotte fell asleep almost at once on the thick carpet of fragrant pine branches which covered the floor of the wigwam. Soon Mère Marie was also deep in slumber. Nevertheless, she was awake and ready long before the first rays of dawn were tinging the misty waters of the Saint Lawrence in glorious shades of rose and gold. Ah, how good to be alive on this first day of August 1639! To know that it was almost time to begin the work of saving souls that God had destined for her—the dream that had burned in her heart for so many years!

The travelers did reach Quebec by eight o'clock that same morning. And what a welcome awaited them in the little village! Church bells rang, cannon boomed, and the entire population of two hundred men, women and children cheered themselves hoarse as Governor Charles de Montmagny approached the water's edge and prepared to deliver his official greeting.

"I can see the nuns, Maman!" cried one eight-year-old girl excitedly. "They've got on muddy black dresses!"

"No, no, Yvette!" protested a six-year-old brother. "They've got on muddy white dresses!"

"Sssh, nuns don't wear white, Michel."

"They do, too."

"They don't!"

"They do!"

The children's mother, tears of happiness streaming down her face, hugged the little ones to her. "Sssh, my children, you're both right," she said quickly. "The nuns in black are Ursulines, who'll be teaching school here. The nuns in white are Augustinians, who'll be nursing the sick. How lucky we are to have them in Quebec!"

Suddenly the children's eyes grew round with

THE GOVERNOR PREPARED TO DELIVER
HIS OFFICIAL GREETING.

wonder. The nuns in black and the nuns in white, having now stepped ashore, were kneeling to kiss the ground! And two ladies who seemed to be their friends were doing the same.

"Why are the nuns and the ladies kissing the ground?" demanded little Michel excitedly. "Does it mean something special, Maman?"

The mother nodded through her tears. "Of course, son. It means they love our new country very much, and everyone who lives in it. It means they want to help us to make Canada a really holy place."

Greatly impressed, the children listened quietly as Governor de Montmagny began his address of welcome. But when the ceremony was over, they tugged eagerly at their mother's skirts. Couldn't they see the nuns and the ladies at closer range, they wanted to know. Couldn't they have a few words with them?

"Not now, dears. We're going to church."

"Church! But why, Maman?"

"Because the good nuns and the ladies want to hear Mass and receive Holy Communion. Tomorrow, perhaps, when they've rested a bit, we might be able to have a visit with them."

Greatly disappointed, Yvette and Michel joined in the procession that was now preparing to leave for Notre Dame de la Recouvrance, the little chapel where Samuel de Champlain had loved to pray. However, they had gone but a few steps when their eyes brightened. One of the Ursulines had just smiled and waved at them! And Père Paul Le Jeune, hurrying to join his fellow Jesuits, had stopped for a brief greeting.

"Well, little ones, Mère Marie de l'Incarnation seems to have taken a fancy to you," he observed jovially. "And that's good, for she's a very holy woman."

The children were delighted. So Mère Marie was the name of their unknown friend. And she was very holy.

"Could we see her, Father? Today?"

The children's mother was embarrassed. What a time for idle chatter, with the procession about to begin! Besides, surely the nuns were too busy getting settled in their new quarters to be able to receive any but the most important visitors?

"Yvette! Michel! What's come over you?" she scolded. "Père Le Jeune can't talk with us now. And haven't I already said that we'll try to see the nuns tomorrow?"

The superior of the Jesuits (whose *Relation* of 1635 had strengthened Mère Marie in her desire to come to Canada) laid his hands playfully on the children's heads. "There, now, Madame, it's all right," he said, smiling. "I always have time for the little ones. And I think that this afternoon Mère Marie will have time for them, too. I'll ask her about it as soon as Mass is over."

Busy though she was, Mère Marie did have time to chat with Yvette and Michel that afternoon, and with other friends of Père Le Jeune as well. But when the long day was finally over—with its speeches, feasting, sight-seeing and fireworks—she could not bring herself to relax. Nor could her companions.

"Goodness, I've scarcely had a chance to look about," said Mère Cécile when the last visitor had departed from the little house on the waterfront which was to be their temporary home. "What do we have, anyway?"

Madame de la Peltrie burst out laughing. "Not much, Mother. Just a flimsy two-room cottage hanging onto the cliff above the river. But of course we'll build a proper convent later on."

"High up on the rock near the Governor's residence at Fort Saint Louis?"

"Yes, we'll have a house on the rock, God willing."

Mère Saint Joseph's eyes twinkled. "In the meantime, don't make fun of 'The Louvre,'" she warned.

"The Louvre?"

"Yes, Madame. That's what I'm calling this little place, after the famous palace in France. You see, I plan to be as happy as a queen here."

Charlotte nodded eagerly. "So do I. Besides, has the real Louvre a view to compare with ours? Just look!"

One by one the group crossed to the window and peered outside. Darkness had long since fallen on the great rock where Samuel de Champlain had founded the settlement of Quebec some thirty-one years before. Now, however, a newly risen moon was casting a luminous sheen over the full breadth of the mighty Saint Lawrence. Scarcely two hundred yards away, directly below their little house, the

Saint Jacques and other ships rode lazily at anchor, while across the river to the south loomed a vast wilderness of forest, black and mysterious in the soft August night. Someday, two hundred feet up the sheer cliff at their backs, they would have larger quarters, but surely no greater happiness than that of the present moment.

"Quebec!" thought Mère Marie, tears of joy filling her eyes as she gazed with the others at the peaceful scene. "Years ago God showed you to me in a dream—your rivers, your forests, your rocks, your lights and shadows. But you were never this beautiful—never, never!"

CHAPTER 7

NEW FRANCE

EARLY THE next morning the hospital nuns, who had temporary quarters near the fort, accompanied their Ursuline friends to Sillery. Here, some four miles from Quebec, the Jesuits were teaching various trades to a number of Indian converts and converts-to-be. Land had been cleared, garden plots laid out, workshops set up—and a fine chapel now graced the center of the little colony.

"What a beautiful place!" exclaimed Mère Marie, when Père Le Jeune had finished showing them around. "And how well the little ones sing their hymns and say their prayers! Tell me, Father, are there other Christian villages like this in Canada?"

The priest smiled. "A few. But a place like Sillery isn't the complete answer to the problem, Mère Marie. The Indians are a wandering race. Most of them would rather be free to roam the woods and exist on whatever game and fish they can find than live in a village and work at farming or a trade."

Mère Marie grew thoughtful. "But if the Indian

converts don't stay in one place, Father, where they can hear Mass regularly and receive the Sacraments, won't they fall away from the Faith? Won't they become just as pagan as their brothers in the woods?"

The Jesuit shrugged and sighed. "That's what's happened more than once, even though all our converts have to go through a long period of trial before we'll let them be baptized. However, from now on there may be a change for the better. If you can train the Indian children while they're still very young to know and love God, they'll want to keep the Catholic Faith no matter where they go."

That very day, to the Ursulines' great delight, a newly baptized Algonquin girl from Sillery was given into their care. She was ten-year-old Marie, whose parents had been most favorably impressed by the French ladies and the nuns. Now they were sure that their child could learn a great deal, and be happy, too, if she went to live at the new convent in Quebec.

"What a darling you are, Marie!" exclaimed Mère Marie, as she hugged the solemn-eyed little girl to herself in greeting. Then to Charlotte she went on, "I can hardly wait to get back home and give her some pretty clothes."

Charlotte was amused. "We'd best have her wash first, though, Mother. The poor child is covered with bear grease, just like the little Indians in Tadoussac. And she has fleas, too."

Mère Marie shrugged. Who cared about bear grease or fleas, when the newly baptized Marie had a soul that was as pure as snow? "I want to take a second child, too," she said eagerly, "just in case Marie gets lonesome."

Père Le Jeune chuckled. "Slowly, Mother," he cautioned. "I think we'd better see how this little one does before we send you more children."

A few weeks later, though, when smallpox broke out in Sillery, these words were forgotten. Dozens of panic-stricken Indians were streaming into Quebec for treatment. The hospital nuns cared for as many of these as they could, but soon the Ursulines were also called upon to help. Indeed, by mid-November the little house on the riverfront was crowded to the doors with sick and dying.

"Father in Heaven, what can we do for these poor people?" sighed Mère Cécile, as she went about making up one bed after another on the bare floor. "If only we were nurses, Mère Marie, or had the proper medicines and supplies. But this way, with scarcely any equipment, and no experience at all—"

Mère Marie refused to worry. "God will use our love and prayers," she said cheerfully. "I'm sure of that. Wasn't this a golden opportunity to help bring these precious souls to Our Lord?"

By the end of February, 1640, Mère Marie and the nuns of her community had nursed back to health all but four of their unexpected guests, and these four had been baptized before they died. And even more: in spite of all their labors for the sick and dying, Madame de la Peltrie, Charlotte and the nuns had made excellent progress in learning the

Algonquin and Huron languages. Mère Marie and Mère Saint Joseph were already giving several little Indians catechism lessons in these difficult tongues. Also, they were teaching them to read, to write and to sew.

"Surely the Holy Spirit is helping these good women!" observed a certain Jesuit priest one day. "Why, it took me nearly a year to master just one little prayer in Algonquin—the Sign of the Cross!"

His companion, a young lay brother, nodded ruefully. "It took me longer than that," he sighed. "Yet weeks before Christmas, Mère Marie and Mère Saint Joseph knew all the prayers in the catechism, even the Apostles' Creed. I tell you, Father, I do believe that miracles are going on in that little house of theirs down by the river. Real miracles!"

The people of Quebec agreed. Now that the Indians were away in the woods on the winter hunt, their children and womenfolk were packing the little convent to the doors. True, at first most of these guests had been more interested in receiving free food, clothing and shelter than in learning about the Faith. Gradually, though, the charity of Mère Marie and her companions had touched their hearts.

The weeks passed and the first signs of spring began to appear along the Saint Lawrence. In spite of the smallpox plague, the bitter cold and a monotonous diet of eels, salt pork and codfish, they were all in excellent health. Even Mère Saint Joseph, whose frailty had so often alarmed the superiors in France, was strong and well.

"Goodness, it'll be summer before we know it!" Madame de la Peltrie told Charlotte one bright morning in early April, as they went for a brief walk about Quebec. "See? Already the ice is breaking in the river."

The girl looked. Along the entire stretch of the Saint Lawrence, frozen almost solid since the previous November, enormous mounds of ice were grinding their way downstream with a deafening roar. Nearer at hand, on the narrow beach below the great rock of Quebec, a lone fisherman was mending his boat.

Charlotte took a deep breath of the clean, fresh air. "What a fine sight, Madame! Still, can't you think of one you'd like better?"

Madame de la Peltrie laughed. "Of course. Everyone longs to see the river entirely free of ice, and the ships from home making their way into port."

"Is it true that we can't expect them until June or July?"

"I'm afraid so, my dear."

Charlotte sighed. "Eight months is a long, long time to have to wait for news from France!"

"It is indeed, especially when we remember that some of the ships may not reach here at all. They could be captured by pirates, or else crushed by icebergs. For that reason, I think we ought to ask the little Indian children to pray for the safe arrival of the fleet. Marie, Agnès, Thérèse, Louise, Madeleine, Marie-Ursule—ah, surely they'll be glad to offer an extra Hail Mary every day for this intention?"

Madame de la Peltrie was right. The six Indian youngsters who were now staying at the convent were more than willing to pray for the safe arrival of the French ships. And the children's faith was rewarded. On a warm day in late June, far down the river near the Ile d'Orléans, the residents of Quebec caught the glint of strange white sails against the horizon. A few days later, even as they were still rejoicing over the arrival of the first ships from home, the rest of the fleet came into port.

To Mère Marie the *Espérance*, which had arrived at Quebec on July 8, brought not only food but medicine and other supplies for her little family. It also brought two good helpers from the Ursuline convent in Paris: Mères Anne de Sainte Claire and Marguerite de Saint Athanase. There were several encouraging letters from Claude, too, who was now back at the Jesuit school in Orléans. Once again he was doing well with his studies, he wrote. And though Aunt Claude still refused to take an interest in him, Monsieur de Bernières and others were proving to be very good friends. There was not the slightest need to worry about his future.

"Dear Lord, how can I thank You for all these blessings?" thought Mère Marie, as she settled herself to read her boy's letters still another time.

Mère Marie's companions rejoiced with her at the good news from Claude. And as for the exciting rumor which the Paris Ursulines had brought with them—that next year several men and women would found a colony in Our Lady's honor a hundred and fifty miles farther up the Saint Lawrence—on a densely wooded island known as Montreal—

"It's almost too good to be true!" exclaimed Madame de la Peltrie, her eyes alight. "Tell me, Mothers, who has charge of this venture?"

Exhausted though they were after their long sea voyage, the newly arrived Ursulines hastened to satisfy her curiosity. Details were still lacking, they said, but in Dieppe it was believed that Monsieur Paul de Chomédy de Maisonneuve, only twenty-eight years old, would head the proposed colony at Montreal. Also, that thirty-three-year-old Mademoiselle Jeanne Mance would assist him.

At once Madame de la Peltrie was alive with interest. Paul de Maisonneuve and Jeanne Mance! Now, what could she do to help these two brave souls?

As the months passed, Père Barthélemy Vimont remarked Madame de la Peltrie's increasing interest in the new colony at Montreal. Though he had now replaced Père Le Jeune as superior of the Jesuit missions in Canada, he still found time to visit the Ursulines' little house and to discuss various problems with Mère Marie.

"I do believe our good friend would like to go to Montreal," he observed one day. "She's a real apostle, you know, afraid of nothing."

Mère Marie's dark eyes became anxious. "That's true, Father," she admitted. "But what about the work here? Madame de la Peltrie laid the first stone for our new convent near Fort Saint Louis just a few weeks ago, and the building should be finished by the end of next year. But if she's now decided to withdraw her support—"

The Jesuit smiled. "I don't think she'll do that, Mother—not when she gave her word to finance the first school for girls in North America. What she may do is to build the convent here, a chapel in Montreal, then try to divide her time between the two."

Mère Marie shook her head. "It's not safe for Madame de la Peltrie to go to Montreal," she protested. "Why, there's not yet even a settlement there, let alone a fort and soldiers to protect her from the Iroquois!"

Père Vimont thought back. Even before the arrival of the Paris Ursulines, he had known about that remarkable group in France, "The Gentlemen and Ladies of the Society of Our Lady of Montreal," which had long been preparing to establish a Christian settlement, similar to that of Quebec, on the island of Montreal. Now, if the Society had actually engaged the services of the experienced soldier Paul de Maisonneuve to head this venture, there was surely no need to worry about a lack of military protection for the colonists. He would build an adequate fort at Montreal.

"Perhaps we're just borrowing trouble," he said finally. "If Madame de la Peltrie does leave us— well, the future is in God's hands, not ours."

Mère Marie became more cheerful. "Of course, Father! Then, too, Madame de la Peltrie may lose interest in Montreal even before Monsieur de Maisonneuve and Mademoiselle Mance arrive. Or perhaps there'll be a change of plans, and they won't come at all."

On August 8, 1641, however, Mademoiselle Mance and several Montreal colonists landed at Quebec. And no sooner had Mère Marie laid eyes on Mademoiselle Jeanne than she felt herself drawn in an extraordinary fashion to this radiant young woman.

"Welcome, my dear!" Mère Marie cried eagerly, throwing wide her arms. "A thousand welcomes to New France!"

Mademoiselle Jeanne quickly returned the warm embrace. "How good to see you, Mère Marie!" she exclaimed, tears of joy welling from her dark eyes. "You'll never know how many times I've dreamed of this happy day!"

Two months later, when the storm-tossed vessel bearing Monsieur de Maisonneuve and his followers also reached port, all Quebec had fallen in love with Jeanne Mance. What courage she had, what love of souls, to want to go into the dangerous country along the upper Saint Lawrence and help to found a colony! As for the newly arrived Paul de Maisonneuve, smiling and cheerful in spite of months of the most dreadful hardships at sea—ah, he, too, was taken to their hearts. . . .

From the beginning, however, Governor de Montmagny warned the newcomers that he did not approve of their venture. The friendly Hurons who lived on the unfortified island of Montreal were frequently set upon by the Iroquois. Then, what dreadful massacres and destruction! What suffering

"A THOUSAND WELCOMES TO NEW FRANCE!"

for young and old!

"Since the Iroquois are also our enemies, Monsieur," the Governor told De Maisonneuve frankly, "you'd do much better to settle close to Quebec. Then, in times of danger, our two settlements could present a united front. Now, what do you say to building your colony on the Ile d'Orléans, just seven miles from here? The soil is rich, with a fine stand of timber, and it's yours for the asking."

De Maisonneuve hesitated. Should he try to explain to the Governor that in a vision on February 2, 1630, at La Flèche, France, a holy man named Jérôme le Royer de la Dauversière had been told to found an order of hospital nuns, then to establish a settlement at Montreal as a site for their labors? That, as a result, the newly arrived colonists were pledged to build a town at Montreal and nowhere else in Canada? Ah, no! The story was too long and complicated. On the other hand, since the Governor was plainly trying to be helpful—

"Monsieur, I do appreciate your point of view," he said courteously. "It would be good for us to be neighbors. And with all my heart I thank you for the generous offer of land. Still, my decision stands. We go up to Montreal at once."

The Governor's eyes narrowed. What nonsense was this? "But I've already told you that Montreal is in dangerous country," he protested, "that you and your colonists could be wiped out in a single Iroquois attack. Are you going to argue with one who knows New France as I do?"

De Maisonneuve bowed politely. "I am not here

to argue, Monsieur, but to act. Believe me, if all the trees at Montreal should turn into Iroquois, I'd still go there to found my colony."

In spite of himself, the Governor was impressed. And though he was still beset by doubts, he finally agreed to go with De Maisonneuve to Montreal. They would look over the island together and make plans for the future. The trip must be a quick one, of course, since winter was at hand. Also, only the hardiest of the colonists were to go along. The others, including Jeanne Mance, would remain in Quebec and try to find temporary quarters for the entire group.

"That may be difficult, since you have some fifty persons in your party," warned the Governor. "After all, with accommodations so scarce here—"

De Maisonneuve smiled and shrugged. "The Lord will provide for us, Monsieur," he said cheerfully. "Wait and see."

His faith was rewarded. When the pioneers returned to Quebec in late October, they found that an elderly man, Pierre de Puiseaux, had become so interested in their project that he was now turning over to them as winter quarters his two fine country houses near Quebec. Even more. In the spring, when the Saint Lawrence was free of ice, the seventy-five-year-old benefactor would give them the rest of his worldly goods and go along with them to Montreal.

Before the week was out, the Montreal colonists were happily settled in their new quarters—De Maisonneuve, Jeanne Mance and several other men and women in the De Puiseaux home at Saint Michel, near Sillery, the remainder at nearby Saint Foy. Needless to say, Pierre de Puiseaux tried hard to make his new friends feel at home. The best food and drink were theirs for the asking, and soon all Quebec admitted that the old man seemed to have found his youth again. He was up at dawn with his fifty guests, joining in their prayers, their discussions, their labors, and going to bed only when they themselves were exhausted.

"Why, the good soul is even letting them cut down his best trees at Saint Foy so they can build ships for the trip to Montreal in the spring," one person told another incredulously.

"Really? I never thought he'd be that generous!"

"Neither did I."

"And Madame de la Peltrie! She's spending half her time at Saint Michel, helping Jeanne Mance and the other women with their sewing."

"Poor Mère Marie! I wonder what she thinks about all this?"

Much as she admired Paul de Maisonneuve and Jeanne Mance and wished them well, Mère Marie was sick at heart over Madame de la Peltrie's continued preoccupation with their work. Could it be that Père Vimont's fears were justified, that she would be off to Montreal in the spring with her new friends? What a blow that would be! Yet when she remembered the wonderful news that the colonists' ships had brought the previous summer—that on January 15, 1641, Claude had joined the Benedictines of Saint Maur and was now extremely happy as a novice at Vendôme—she knew she would carry her cross in silence.

"Father in Heaven, through the merits of this little suffering joined to the great sufferings of Your Son, let my son persevere in his new life," she prayed. "Let him be a priest someday, a truly holy priest. . . ."

Gradually Mère Marie experienced new peace of soul. There were even times when she wondered if her present cross would not soon be removed. Spring was at hand, the spring of 1642. Perhaps Madame de la Peltrie would not go to Montreal after all. Yet—

"My God, whatever You wish," she prayed again, summoning all her courage. "With Your help, I'll suffer anything for the sake of my son. . . ."

And then it happened—on a brisk day in early March. Greatly embarrassed, and with many apologies, Madame de la Peltrie confided to Mère Marie that she now felt certain God wanted her to work for souls in Montreal. The building of the new convent high upon the rock of Quebec would still be her responsibility, of course, but she could not afford to maintain it when it had been completed.

"You're not angry with me, Mother?" she asked anxiously. "And you won't mind if I take Charlotte to Montreal? And the dishes and furniture that I brought from France?"

Mère Marie smiled bravely. "Of course not, my dear. You're to do whatever you think best."

"But I was so afraid—"

"Why should you be? Your good friends need all the help you can give them."

Instantly Madame de la Peltrie's blue eyes brightened. "What a relief to hear you say that!" she burst out gratefully. "This is wonderful, Mère Marie! How good you are. . . ."

CHAPTER 8

THE HOUSE FOR JESUS AND MARY

ON MAY 8, however, when Madame de la Peltrie and Charlotte set out for Montreal with De Maisonneuve and his colonists, taking along nearly all that Madame possessed, Mère Cécile's heart was heavy. The little house on the riverfront had always been a poor place, of course, but now—

"Only three beds left!" she told Mère Marie mournfully. "Good heavens, Mother, where are we going to put our fourteen little Indian girls tonight, not to mention ourselves?"

Mère Marie tried to be cheerful. "We'll manage somehow," she said quickly. "And we mustn't think harshly of our good friend, my dear. After all, she does have the right to live where she pleases."

"But to take the best dishes, towels, sheets, blankets, pots and pans, Mother! As well as the beds!"

Mère Saint Joseph's eyes twinkled. "Did you forget that all these things really belong to Madame de la Peltrie?" she chided playfully. "Let's just be

98

grateful that she didn't take the house, too."

"Now you're making fun of me!"

"Well—"

Mère Anne de Sainte Claire, of the Paris Ursulines, smiled and shrugged. "Let's not worry about
anything," she urged. "After all, we're no poorer
than Our Lady was on the first Christmas night.
Besides, surely we can borrow some odds and ends
from the neighbors?"

"Of course," said Mère Marguerite de Saint
Athanase, her fellow Parisian. "Then, too, the ships
will soon be coming with fresh supplies. Ah, Mère
Cécile, just wait and see if everything doesn't turn
out well."

She was right. Even before the day was over, people were coming to the convent with what they
could spare of furniture, dishes, linen and bedding.
Some were inclined to be critical of Madame de
la Peltrie, even of Paul de Maisonneuve and Jeanne
Mance, but Mère Marie refused to listen to any
uncharitable remarks. The Montreal colonists were
good and holy people, she said, and were doing
God's work as they saw fit.

"Madame de la Peltrie will be really happy helping to found a settlement at Montreal," she said
kindly. "And so will Charlotte."

Still, Mère Marie could not help worrying about
the Montreal colonists. As the weeks passed, there
were constant rumors that the Iroquois had left
their haunts south of the Saint Lawrence and were
planning to attack the Hurons, their sworn enemies. Since Montreal was in Huron country, she

prayed no harm would come to her good friends.

Her concern was justified. In the late fall of that same year, 1642, dreadful news was brought to Governor de Montmagny. On August 2, it seemed, some thirty-one miles north of the settlement of Trois Rivières, young Dr. René Goupil, who had been donating his medical services to the Jesuits for the past two years, had been captured by the Iroquois. His companions, Père Isaac Jogues and Guillaume Couture, had also been taken, together with several Huron converts. And what torments the little group had suffered! Indeed, on September 29 poor Dr. Goupil had been done to death by the Iroquois at the early age of thirty-four. As for Père Jogues and Guillaume Couture, after unspeakable tortures they had been made the slaves of the Iroquois womenfolk. Now no one knew their whereabouts, or what other sufferings they were being forced to endure.

Mère Marie could scarcely believe the dreadful news. To think that Dr. Goupil and Père Jogues, who had so often visited at the convent, should have been captured and tortured by the Iroquois! And this, less than seventy miles from Montreal!

"The same thing could have happened to Madame de la Peltrie and Charlotte," she told herself, shuddering. "Surely they ought to be brought back right away?"

But neither the pleas of Governor de Montmagny nor those of Père Vimont could sway the courageous Madame de la Peltrie. What nonsense to say that Montreal was a dangerous place, she wrote. So far not even Pilote, the colonists' pet dog, had seen an Iroquois. Instead, there were only friendly Hurons—hundreds of them—anxious to hear about God. Truly, Montreal was a wonderful place. Mère Marie ought to come there at once and open a school for the children.

When she had finished reading Madame de la Peltrie's letter, Mère Saint Joseph burst out laughing. The Ursulines should open a school in Montreal when they could scarcely support the one they already had in Quebec!

"Our good friend does have remarkable faith," she chuckled. "When do we leave, Mother?"

Mère Marie shook her head. "This is no laughing matter, my dear. Madame de la Peltrie doesn't begin to realize her grave danger. Let's ask the first of our Jesuit martyrs in Canada to bring her back to us."

"Dr. René Goupil?"

"That's right. Of course the good young doctor wasn't actually a Jesuit, only a lay helper, but he died because of his missionary work with them. Surely God will hear his prayers for Madame de la Peltrie and Charlotte?"

By mid-November, however, as the waters of the Saint Lawrence turned to ice, Mère Marie sadly admitted that her two friends would not be coming back that year. This was doubly disappointing, since on November 21 the community planned to move to the fine new convent—the house on the rock—which Madame de la Peltrie's generosity had provided for them.

"It's all right, Mother," said Père Vimont consolingly. "Madame de la Peltrie and Charlotte will be with us in spirit on that day."

"And René Goupil, too," added Soeur Saint Laurent, a young lay Sister who had arrived from Dieppe during the past summer. "Ah, we mustn't let anything spoil our great day!"

In spite of herself, Mère Marie smiled. How good to have still another helper from France! "Come, now, Sister, don't tell me we should set aside all our troubles on November 21," she said with mock concern.

Soeur Saint Laurent nodded eagerly. "Oh, yes, Mother! And not just on that one day, but on every day of the year. It's what René Goupil would want of us."

"Sister! Who told you that?"

"No one, Mère Marie. I just feel it in my heart."

"But—"

"When the good young doctor lived on earth, he helped everyone who came to him. Now that he lives in Heaven—"

"He can do still more?"

"Yes. If we have real faith, René Goupil will ask the good God to let him work all kinds of wonders for us. And can the good God fail to listen to one who gave Him everything, even life itself?"

The words of Soeur Saint Laurent were a real consolation to Mère Marie. Indeed, in the chill dawn of November 21, as she and her companions climbed silently up the one narrow path in Quebec that led to their new home, her heart was filled with gratitude. What had seemed so impossible seven years before—the house on the rock for Jesus and Mary—was now an accomplished fact. True, there was still much work to be done on the interior of the new convent. Undoubtedly they would also know many hardships behind those sturdy walls. Yet weren't these part of the price to be paid for a fruitful work among the people of New France? Even for her own son's glorious vocation to the priesthood as a Benedictine monk? Of course!

Later in the day, crowds of well-wishers climbed the same steep path to see for themselves the imposing stone convent that stood near Fort Saint Louis, the Governor's residence, atop the great rock of Quebec. Ninety-two feet long, twenty-eight feet wide, three stories high, with a magnificent view of the Saint Lawrence, it was truly the finest building in New France. And to everyone's amazement there was a place in the still unfinished chapel for a shrine to the Sacred Heart of Jesus.

"My, I wonder if there's another such shrine in the whole world," said one woman. "Certainly Mère Marie's the first person I ever knew who thought of paying honor to Jesus in His Sacred Heart."

Her companion was thoughtful. "God seems to have chosen her to make this devotion known to priests and layfolk alike, especially here in Canada."

"How wonderful! Still, why do you suppose she has such great faith in the devotion?"

"Well, they do say that while she was living in

Tours, and worrying about how she was to begin her work in Canada, she heard God speaking in the depths of her soul. *'Ask Me by the Heart of Jesus, My most beloved Son,'* He told her. *'Through Him I will hear you and grant you your requests.'"*

"Isn't that a great sign of favor from Heaven?"

"Of course."

"Then Mère Marie's a saint?"

"The Jesuit Fathers think so. They even say that someday the whole world will want to know all about her and the wonderful work she's been doing here in Quebec."

Although the care and education of Indian girls had been the Ursulines' chief task, they had also accepted as boarders two motherless French girls—fourteen-year-old Madeleine Nicolet and fifteen-year-old Marie Olivier. Following the move to the new convent, they enrolled twelve or so additional French girls as students.

"How good to have all these new pupils!" Mère Marie told Père Vimont one bright September morning in the year 1643. "Now, if only Madame de la Peltrie would come back to help with the teaching. . .and Charlotte, too."

The priest smiled. "That may happen sooner than you think," he said cheerfully.

Mère Marie was startled. "Father! You don't mean—"

"I do, Mother. Governor de Montmagny has just sent word for our two good friends to return here at once."

"He—he thinks the Iroquois will attack Montreal this winter?"

"He does."

"But Madame de la Peltrie will just laugh at the Governor's order, Father! She's done that before, you know. Many times."

"True, but this time should be different."

"Different! How different?"

Père Vimont shrugged. "Remember how the Montreal colonists always admired Madame de la Peltrie's eagerness to convert the Indians? Well, they still do. But now that she wants to take a canoe and go off into the deep woods as a missionary—to leave the safety of De Maisonneuve's fort and live with the Hurons in one of their own villages—well, that's too much. Even Jeanne Mance will be relieved to have her return to Quebec."

Sudden tears filled Mère Marie's dark eyes. "But she will be heartbroken about all this!" she exclaimed. "She'll consider herself a failure for the rest of her days!"

"Oh, no, I don't think so," put in one of the other nuns. "I believe that Madame de la Peltrie will realize she tried her best but it simply didn't work out. And certainly it's not like she won't have any important work to do helping with conversions here in Quebec."

The speaker proved a true prophet. Some two months later, accompanied by the faithful Charlotte, Madame de la Peltrie returned to Quebec. She was in high spirits and had enjoyed every minute of her eighteen-month stay in Montreal, she assured the Ursulines. Now that wonderful adventure was over, and it seemed God wanted her to live in Quebec after all.

"How good to see you, Mère Marie!" she exclaimed, her blue eyes dancing with excitement. "And the new convent! Do you like it, my dear? Is it large enough? Have you plenty of supplies? Are my little Indians well and happy?"

Mère Marie was overwhelmed. So Madame de la Peltrie had not lost interest in the Quebec project after all! She was really eager to be of help, just as in the old days.

Before the week was out, the newcomers were happily settled in their former way of life. Scores of old friends came to wish them well, and to hear of Madame de la Peltrie's plans for building her own home as soon as spring came. It would, she said, be just a small house on the convent grounds, but visitors would always be welcome.

This news was of immediate interest to all the little Indian girls. "Could we come and visit your new house, too?" they asked eagerly.

Madame de la Peltrie smiled. "Of course, my dears, whenever Mère Marie says that you may."

"You'll have parties for us?"

"Why not?"

"With caraway-seed cakes and candies?"

"And hot chocolate to drink?"

Madame de la Peltrie burst out laughing. "Of course! I'll have all those good things for you, my children, and many more, too."

Marie Madeleine de la Peltrie was true to her

word. Many a gay frolic was held for the Indian children in her house, followed by excursions to Sillery and other points in and about Quebec.

One morning, however, as Père Jérôme Lalemant was giving the little Indians their usual catechism lesson, he was more than puzzled. How sad everyone looked!

"What's the trouble?" he asked kindly. "Don't you want to hear about Jesus today?"

Eight-year-old Marie-Ursule gazed mournfully at the floor. "We. . .we always want to h-hear about Jesus," she said in a choked voice. "He loves us, even if we d-don't have pretty c-clothes. . . ."

"L-like the French g-girls," sniffed Nicole, another eight-year-old.

Père Lalemant stared in amazement. Why, Marie-Ursule and Nicole were almost in tears! And some of the other little girls, too!

"There, now, what our bodies look like doesn't matter nearly so much as what our souls look like," he said cheerfully. "Let's just remember that if we say our prayers well, and do our work well, our souls will be more beautiful in God's sight than the sun or the moon or the stars. Isn't that wonderful?"

The children looked at one another. What Père Lalemant said was true, of course. Still, wouldn't it be nice to have a pretty red dress like Marguerite's? Shiny black shoes like Geneviève's? New wool stockings like Elisabeth's?

"Of course it would!" exclaimed Mère Marie, when she had heard about what had happened in the classroom. "Poor little things, I had no idea that they felt like this."

The Jesuit hesitated. "Frankly, I'm upset," he declared, frowning. "These children should be more grateful for all that we've done for them. Aren't their clothes clean and warm, even if they did come secondhand from France two years ago?"

Mère Marie's eyes twinkled. "Yes, Father, but I'm afraid you don't understand little girls."

"What?"

"They all love pretty clothes."

"But—"

"Look, Father, there's some good red serge in the storeroom. I'll start right away to make the children new dresses. And I'll try to get them new shoes and stockings as well."

Soon all the Indian children had fine new outfits. A special party was arranged for them, too, at which Soeur Saint Laurent provided a generous assortment of goodies, including a huge platter of caraway-seed cakes, their favorite treat. As a climax, Mère Saint Joseph brought her viol to the dining room, and soon a dozen little red-clad figures, their bronzed faces shining with excitement, were singing and dancing to a variety of lively French airs.

"Aren't they having the best time?" laughed Mère Marie, as she and Madame de la Peltrie stood watching the happy scene. "It does me a world of good just to be here."

Madame de la Peltrie nodded eagerly. "It does me good, too, Mother. And to think that this is only the beginning of our work! There'll be many more little ones to care for as time goes on—that is, if

SOON THEY WERE SINGING AND DANCING
TO A VARIETY OF LIVELY FRENCH AIRS.

the Iroquois will just leave us in peace."

For a moment Mère Marie's dark eyes grew troubled. The Iroquois! Who could trust them? Or tell their plans? True, poor Guillaume Couture, whom they had taken prisoner more than two years before, had finally been allowed his freedom. And his fellow sufferer, Père Isaac Jogues, had somehow managed to escape their clutches and was now safe in Montreal. On the other hand—

"Well, let's leave the future to Divine Providence," she said, after a moment's reflection. "Who knows? God may give the poor Iroquois the gift of faith far sooner than we think."

In the days that followed, however, when Madame de la Peltrie and Charlotte had moved into their new house on the convent grounds, there were many who wondered just how long they would be content to stay. After all, Madame de la Peltrie was not a nun, with vows, but a wealthy and independent woman who thrived on adventure. Since neither the Jesuits nor Governor de Montmagny would hear of her going off to be a missionary on her own—

"The poor soul will soon tire of just praying for the Iroquois and making sacrifices for their conversion," one person told another.

"It seems likely. She'll doubtless decide to give up her quiet life and return to France."

"Still, what about Charlotte?"

"Why, she'll go along, too, of course."

"What if she'd like to marry and settle down here?"

"Impossible! Charlotte would never leave Madame de la Peltrie for anyone or anything on earth. She'll stay with her until she dies."

In the summer of 1647, however, there was astonishing news. Twenty-seven-year-old Charlotte Barré was about to become an Ursuline! And forty-five-year-old Madame de la Peltrie also was thinking of entering the cloister.

"Heavens!" exclaimed Père Lalemant, when Mère Marie had brought him word of this. "Madame de la Peltrie hasn't the slightest vocation to the religious life! Her age, her temperament, everything's against her. Yet since it's her money that built the new convent—well, what are you going to tell her?"

Mère Marie smiled and shrugged. "The truth, Father."

"You think she'll understand?"

"I'm sure she will. She's really very humble, you know, in spite of her impetuous ways. And holy, too."

Poor Madame de la Peltrie! When she learned that the Ursulines did not think she should join their ranks, she was greatly discouraged. Life without Charlotte was so humdrum and lonely!

"It's hard to be all alone in the world," she told Mère Marie one day. "What am I going to do with myself?"

Mère Marie embraced her good friend warmly. "You're going to be a saint, my dear. A great saint."

Madame de la Peltrie smiled ruefully. "A great saint? All alone in my little house?"

"There, now, you'll stay with us whenever you wish. And let's remember that God's plans always work out perfectly, especially if we don't struggle against them."

Slowly Madame de la Peltrie's blue eyes began to brighten. "True, Mother. There's nothing so beautiful as God's will. On the other hand, you must give me plenty of work to do for the Indian children. I'm still useful with a needle, you know. And perhaps I could help out with the teaching now and then?"

"Of course," said Mère Marie kindly. "We'll keep you so busy, my dear, that the time will simply fly for you."

CHAPTER 9

TWO CROSSES

TIME DID fly for Madame de la Peltrie, especially when she finally decided to leave her little house and take up permanent residence with the Ursulines. Indeed, on the bitterly cold evening of December 30, 1650, as she was preparing to retire for the night, she could scarcely realize that more than four years had passed since Charlotte had left her to enter the convent.

"Well, I've managed to get along after all," she told herself happily, as she adjusted the heavy velvet curtains around her bed. "And I've been busy, too, thanks to Mère Marie. What a good friend I've always had in her!"

Soon lights were going out all over the colony as others also sought the haven of their beds against the piercing cold. Nevertheless, the night continued to have a strange radiance all its own. Under the vast December sky, studded with a myriad of glittering stars, the great rock of Quebec loomed starkly beautiful in its thick mantle of snow. And beautiful, too, was the massive iron cross atop the

Ursuline convent, gleaming like a beacon in its armor of ice.

Having taken one last glance at the glorious world outside her window, Madame de la Peltrie settled herself for sleep. How good to have had a hand in the making of New France! To be sharing, even in a small way, in the work of eight saints of God. For by now René Goupil had been joined in martyrdom by seven fellow missionaries: Jean de la Lande, another heroic lay helper, and Père Isaac Jogues, Antoine Daniel, Jean de Brébeuf, Gabriel Lalemant, Charles Garnier and Noël Chabanel.

"Pray for us, O holy martyrs," murmured Madame de la Peltrie sleepily, "that we may be made worthy of the promises of Christ..."

As she drifted into slumber, old memories crowded her mind: memories of girlhood days in Alençon when she had longed to be a nun...of her wealthy father's decision that she marry Charles de la Peltrie instead...of the baby daughter whom God had sent to gladden her days...of the early death of this little one and then of Charles, followed by the loneliness of widowhood, the glorious dream of the pagan Indians in Canada, the heavenly Voice speaking so tenderly in the depths of her soul:

"Will you go and help them?"

"I, Lord? But I'm not worthy!"

"True. But I will use you as My tool. In spite of many obstacles, you will go to Canada and there you will end your days."

As midnight struck, Madame de la Peltrie tossed uneasily in her sleep. The Voice was silent now, but surely there were other voices calling to her in the darkness. Sobbing and frightened voices that told of terrible danger. Then, the convent bell! It, too, seemed to be sounding an alarm...

"W-what is it?" she muttered, as she struggled into wakefulness. "W-what's wrong?"

A moment later her heart all but stopped beating. Why, the convent was on fire! Smoke and flames were everywhere. And clear above the desperate shouts of rescuers stumbling through the snow, the frantic clanging of the tower bell, a chorus of heart-rending screams came from the children's dormitory under the roof!

"I...I'm dreaming!" she gasped in horror. "Dear Father in Heaven, this...this can't be true!"

But it was true. Long before daybreak, though no lives had been lost, the house on the rock lay in smoldering ruins. And as Louis d'Ailleboust, De Montmagny's successor as Governor, finally made his way home to Fort Saint Louis, heartsick and exhausted after hours of rescue work in the bitter cold—

"Well, my dear, it's all over," he told his wife. "The Ursulines have lost everything—convent, chapel, school, furniture, clothes, supplies. Poor Soeur Saint Laurent is simply heartbroken."

Madame d'Ailleboust stared in amazement. "Soeur Saint Laurent! But what has she to do with this awful tragedy?"

Wearily the Governor flung himself into a chair and closed his eyes. "Nothing, really, except that the fire started in the kitchen where she has charge.

THE CONVENT WAS ON FIRE!

It seems that a novice who's been helping her there, Soeur Saint Michel, planned to make bread this morning, and so left a pan of hot coals under the mixing trough last night in order to keep the dough warm."

"Good heavens!"

"Of course Soeur Saint Michel was supposed to make sure that everything was all right before she went to bed, but she forgot. Before midnight the trough caught fire, then the floor, the walls, the ceiling—"

"Oh, Louis, how terrible!"

" 'Terrible' is surely the word, my dear. Now the nuns are poorer than when they first came here eleven years ago. And something tells me that Mère Marie won't have the heart to rebuild. Next summer she'll be returning to France. And the other nuns with her."

During the next three weeks, when she and her fourteen Ursulines were entirely dependent on the hospital nuns for shelter, food and clothing, Mère Marie was inclined to agree with the Governor. How bleak the future looked! She could never arrange for the convent to be rebuilt in the midst of winter, even if funds were available. As for staying on with the hospital nuns, so poor themselves, so pressed for room for the sick and dying—

"Now, Mother, you mustn't worry about anything," said eighteen-year-old Mère Catherine de Saint Augustin, the youngest of the hospital nuns, as they met one morning near the chapel. "We're all so happy to have you here—really! You're not the least bit of trouble."

Mère Marie smiled. What an affectionate little creature Mère Catherine was! And so pretty, too! Yet in spite of her gaiety and youth, she was one of the most efficient workers at the hospital. Indeed, since her arrival at Quebec on the *Cardinal* some two years before, half dead of the plague which had broken out on board, scores of French and Indians had been brought back to health by her marvelous nursing skill.

"Well, my dear, we're really trying not to be a nuisance here," said Mère Marie earnestly. "Still, one of these days I think we'd better leave you."

Mère Catherine stared in dismay. "Leave us, Mother! But where could you go in this bitter cold weather?"

"Perhaps to Madame de la Peltrie's little house. It suffered no damage in the fire, you know. After that? Well, the future is in God's hands. Do pray that we don't question His holy will in any way."

Mère Catherine nodded. "Of course," she said quickly. "And I'll ask my patients to pray, too, especially the children. Poor little things, some of them are very close to God. But do you know something, Mother?"

"What, my dear?"

"You mustn't feel too bad about the fire. After all, the sufferings it brought are only part of God's plan. I know they'll win many blessings for your community in the years ahead. Just wait and see."

As the days passed, Mère Marie often pondered the wisdom in these words. Indeed, in late January,

when she and her little family had finally moved
to Madame de la Peltrie's house—

"Why don't we try to have some of Mère Catherine's beautiful faith?" she asked, smiling. "And why
don't we try to have school again, too?"

Madame de la Peltrie's blue eyes shone. "What
a wonderful idea to bring the children back!" she
exclaimed. "We'll be a bit crowded, of course, but
who minds that? It'll be just like the old days down
by the river."

By mid-April, Marie Madeleine de la Peltrie was
even more pleased. She was playing hostess to fifteen nuns and some thirty French and Indian children, so that now there was never a dull moment
in her little house. And better still, Mère Marie had
decided to rebuild the convent. Where the money
was to come from was a mystery, of course, but
surely God would provide. The main thing, as Mère
Catherine kept reminding them in her cheerful little notes, was for everyone to accept the tragedy
of last December as the will of God. Also, to be
grateful that not a life had been lost in the fire.

"My goodness, I've always been grateful for that,"
Madame de la Peltrie reflected, as she bustled happily about, seeing to the wants of her numerous
household. "It was truly a miracle."

•

Relying on the generosity of friends in France,
Mère Marie went ahead with the rebuilding of the
convent. By February 1652 it was almost ready.
However, Mère Marie herself was sadly troubled
about Mère Saint Joseph, who kept insisting she

would never live to see their new home. She had
not been well even before the fire. When she had
had to leave her sickbed in the freezing cold, clad
only in her night clothes, the shock had been too
much. She had been a semi-invalid ever since.

"I...I know I'm going to die soon," she told the
community one blustery cold day in March.
"You...you will pray for me when I'm gone?"

The nuns looked at one another in dismay. Had
Mère Saint Joseph taken a turn for the worse? Suddenly she seemed so pale, so tired. Then, that terrible weakness in her lungs which made every breath
like a sharp sword thrust...

"Sssh, my dear, you mustn't talk about dying,"
said Mère Cécile soothingly. "Dr. Menouil has
another medicine that should be of real help to
you."

Mère Marie nodded. "That's true, Mother.
Besides, haven't you heard that two new little
Indian girls want to learn to play the viol? You must
get well for their sakes."

Mère Saint Joseph managed a faint smile. "You
do make me feel important," she murmured, "so
wonderfully important! But it's not true, you know.
Not true at all..."

Sudden tears filled Mère Marie's dark eyes. What
a saint Mère Saint Joseph was! Though it had been
impossible to give her a room of her own, because
of the crowded conditions in Madame de la Peltrie's
little house, she had never once complained about
the constant coming and going past the tiny corner
where she lay—the noise from the children's class-

rooms, the heat, the cold, the ever-present kitchen odors, the coughing spells that racked her frail body day and night.

"Father in Heaven, we must do everything possible to keep her with us," Mère Marie reflected. "We must pray as we've never prayed before."

The nuns did pray for Mère Saint Joseph. Indeed, all Quebec was concerned about the young Ursuline's illness. Almost every day the Indians brought choice quail and partridge from the woods, hoping that these delicacies would tempt her failing appetite. The children offered countless sacrifices. As for Madame de la Peltrie, night after night she sat up with the invalid in an effort to amuse her and to ease her pain.

"Well, my dear," she remarked on one of these vigils, "I do believe you're a bit stronger tonight. Here, let me move the candle so I can have a better look."

Mère Saint Joseph smiled faintly. "The candle. . .it scarcely flickers at all, Madame. Such a steady glow it gives. . .not a bit like in the old days. . ."

"The old days?"

"Don't you remember the candles in our first little house down by the river? The wind was always coming through the cracks in the walls and blowing them out, even when we were at our prayers."

Madame de la Peltrie nodded cheerfully. "I remember. And the snow came through the cracks, too, right onto our beds. How long ago it all seems!"

Slowly Mère Saint Joseph closed her eyes. "It was

a long time ago, Madame," she whispered. "I was just twenty-three then. Now I'm thirty-five. . . and dying of tuberculosis. . .of no use to anyone. . ."

"My dear, you mustn't say that!"

"Why not? I can't eat anymore. And yet there was a time when I was always hungry, when I could eat anything. Fish that was half spoiled, eels that were no better, stale bread made from dried peas and corn. . ."

Madame de la Peltrie chuckled. "What about those stews we used to have? Once, when our backs were turned, the little Indian girls threw in a greasy old moccasin for flavoring. And bunches of hair, too. Remember?"

"Yes, I remember. We laughed and laughed about that, then ate every mouthful of the stew because there was nothing else for dinner. But now—"

"What is it, my dear? Do you want something?"

"No, I was just thinking."

"Thinking?"

"About Dom Claude Martin, Mère Marie's son. Hasn't he been a Benedictine priest for more than two years now?"

"Yes, the Bishop ordained him on November 10, 1649, about fourteen months before the fire. Remember how happy we were when the ships brought word of it the next summer?"

But suddenly, like a tired child, Mère Saint Joseph had drifted into sleep. Only when the clock struck midnight did she stir and open her eyes. Then, her face strangely radiant in the dying candlelight, she half rose in her bed.

"What...what time is it in France?" she demanded eagerly.

Startled, Madame de la Peltrie sprang to her feet. "My dear, you mustn't sit up like that in the cold! Here, I'll fetch a blanket—"

"No, no, I'm all right. Tell me, Madame, isn't it five o'clock in the morning in France?"

"Yes. Five o'clock in the morning."

Slowly Mère Saint Joseph settled back against the pillows. "Then Dom Claude is about to remember me at Holy Mass in his monastery," she murmured, her eyes shining. "He's about to beg God to give me a happy death, as Mère Marie asked him to do...my good Mère Marie!"

In the days that followed, Mère Saint Joseph grew steadily weaker. Finally, on April 4 of that same year, 1652, she breathed her last. As her wasted body was taken from Madame de la Peltrie's house to the convent (now completely rebuilt, and even larger and more beautiful than before the fire), Mère Marie smiled bravely through her tears.

"We have a powerful new friend in Heaven," she told her little family, "one who will help us even more than she did on earth."

Mère Cécile choked back a sob. How true this was! Yet the loss of Mère Saint Joseph was a terrible blow for the whole community. What numbers of Indian children, their families and friends, this cheerful little nun had brought to God!

"Father in Heaven, give us faith!" prayed Mère Cécile silently. "Don't let us question Your holy will in any way..."

CHAPTER 10

THE IROQUOIS

THERE WAS good need for Mère Cécile's prayer. Even as Mère Saint Joseph was being laid to rest, the bloodthirsty Iroquois were once again on the warpath. Up and down the Saint Lawrence they ranged, striking terror into every heart as they burned and tortured and killed. Montreal, Trois Rivières, Quebec, the Huron and Algonquin villages—no place was safe from attack.

Nor did the situation improve with the passing of time. Indeed, by May of 1660 the fifth Governor of New France, Pierre d'Argenson, was forced to a desperate decision. Since rumor had it, he said, that at any moment twelve hundred savage Iroquois would be storming Quebec, it was no longer safe for either the Ursuline or the Augustinian nuns to remain in their convents. They must take refuge in the well-fortified house of the Jesuit missionaries. The lay people, equipped with arms and provisions, must also leave their homes for safer quarters in Fort Saint Louis.

Mère Marie's heart sank. Naturally the Governor

124

was anxious to protect his little flock from harm. But surely he didn't mean that she must take refuge with the others? He must certainly agree that the superior of the Ursulines ought to face death in the house on the rock which had cost her so many prayers and sacrifices?

"I'll speak to Bishop de Laval about all this," she decided finally. "He'll understand how I feel."

But the tall and aristocratic thirty-seven-year-old François de Montmorency-Laval, who had come to New France as vicar apostolic only eleven months before, merely smiled and shook his head when Mère Marie had placed her problem before him. "You'd best go with the others, Mother," he said kindly. "Besides, your convent's one of our sturdiest buildings, and close to Fort Saint Louis as well. The Governor wants to make it into a second stronghold."

"But, Monseigneur—"

"After tomorrow, when the Blessed Sacrament is removed and the troops take over, it'll be no fit place for a woman."

Mère Marie hesitated. It seemed unthinkable to turn over the beloved convent to strangers. Yet who was she to argue with the Bishop? Or the Governor either? On the other hand—

"You're right, Monseigneur," she said finally, with surprising meekness. "And the Governor's right, too. Still, isn't it a pity that the soldiers won't be able to do their best for us when the time comes?"

The Bishop stared. "Why, Mother! Every last one of our men will do his best for us! They're heroes—all of them."

"I know, Monseigneur. But even heroes must eat. And unless someone stays in the convent to prepare plenty of nourishing food for the troops—ah, well, the Governor knows best. I'll go now and see about packing my things."

Amusement flickered briefly in the Bishop's shrewd eyes. "Are you joking at such a time, Mother?" he asked, after a moment's reflection. "I never thought about the food problem. And I don't suppose the Governor thought about it either."

Mère Marie's face showed her satisfaction. "You mean you'll ask permission for me to stay and cook for the men, Monseigneur? And for some of the other nuns to help me?"

The Bishop chuckled. Jean de Bernières, one of his best friends in France, and still the generous benefactor of the Ursulines, had told him more than once that if Mère Marie de l'Incarnation could not surmount a difficulty, she always managed to go around it. Well, now he knew that Jean had spoken the truth. Mère Marie was a born leader. And a delightful diplomat as well.

"Don't worry about the Governor, Mother," he said, smiling. "I'm sure he'll agree to what you have in mind."

The Bishop was right. The next day, as the Ursuline and Augustinian communities escorted the Blessed Sacrament to the safety of the Jesuit stronghold, Mère Marie was allowed to remain in her convent with three companions: Charlotte Barré (now Mère Saint Ignace), and Soeurs Sainte

Marthe and Saint Laurent. Of course all four nuns were heavy-hearted, but there was no time for idle grieving. Twenty-four hungry soldiers must be fed before noon, besides the numerous workmen who were now hurriedly boarding up the convent's windows and doors and turning the place into an armed fortress.

"Good heavens, there's a cannon in the chapel already!" exclaimed Mère Saint Ignace, as she set about slicing the bread for dinner. "And twelve huge watchdogs in the garden. Isn't it dreadful to think we may soon have to turn them against our fellow human beings?"

Mère Marie sighed. "It surely is, my dear. But perhaps the Iroquois won't come. If prayers count for anything—"

Soeur Sainte Marthe, busy working in the kitchen at the soup kettle, dabbed at her tear-filled eyes. "Oh," she moaned, "have you seen what the workmen are doing to the floors? Holy Virgin, dirt and fallen plaster everywhere! And the nice finish all scratched. Surely the place will never be the same again."

By nightfall, however, Soeur Sainte Marthe's spirits had risen. The convent was now so well fortified that the Governor and the Bishop had allowed the other nuns to return home. True, they would be going back to the Jesuit house in the morning, and every morning for as long as the danger should last, but at least at night the community could be together as usual.

"How hard our men have worked to make Quebec

safe!" reflected Mère Marie, as she finally settled herself for sleep. "And they did seem to enjoy the two big meals that we cooked for them today. . ."

Yet, as the hours passed, Mère Marie could not relax. In spite of the reassuring presence of the armed guard now silently patrolling the convent grounds, she lay tense and watchful in the soft May night. Dear God, what dreadful days these were for Canada! At any moment, by reason of their superior strength, the Iroquois might destroy both Montreal and Quebec. True, De Maisonneuve had returned four times to France since his arrival in Canada nineteen years ago, and had finally secured a total of some two hundred men to protect his colony at Montreal. He had also acquired the services of a remarkable young school teacher, Marguerite Bourgeoys, who was doing wonders for the French and Indian children there. Three Sulpician priests, the spiritual sons of Jean-Jacques Olier, were also proving their worth at Montreal. And the hospital nuns of Saint Joseph, too, whom Jeanne Mance had brought from La Flèche, when she had visited France the year before.

Yet what was this little group of dedicated men and women when compared with the savage Iroquois hordes? Even Quebec was still no more than a struggling colony, though fifty-two years had passed since it had been founded by Samuel de Champlain.

"Something must be done," murmured Mère Marie wearily, as she finally drifted into slumber. "Something must be done. . ."

The next day, while all continued to brace themselves for the expected Iroquois attack, Bishop de Laval made a thorough inspection of the Ursuline convent. All was in order there: cannon in place, ammunition ready, windows barricaded, the twenty-four soldiers in good spirits, the twelve watchdogs straining at the leash. All doors save one had been boarded over, so that each person entering or leaving the convent could be carefully scrutinized by the sentries.

"Excellent!" the Bishop told Mère Marie, when he had finally completed his rounds. "It's remarkable how much the men have been able to do in such a short time."

Yet the Bishop readily agreed with Mère Marie on the matter so close to her heart. Yes, he said, it was a pity that honest French citizens should have to spend so much time and energy merely to exist in Canada—that they could not serve God, till their lands and raise their families in peace. And why not? Because King Louis XIV, only twenty-two years of age, did not begin to understand the colonists' great need for more protection; that the mere presence of sizable French troops in Canada would immediately make the Iroquois less eager for war.

"If I could, I'd go at once to France and explain matters to His Majesty," said the Bishop thoughtfully. "After all, I do have a few connections at court."

A few connections at court! Mère Marie was filled with admiration of the tall and striking figure beside her. François de Montmorency-Laval, she thought, had a saint's humility, even if he was a member of one of the noblest families in France. Indeed, it was the youthful King Louis himself who, through his mother, Queen Anne of Austria, had suggested three years before to Pope Alexander VII that de Montmorency-Laval would make an excellent bishop for New France.

"Monseigneur, the King would listen to you as to no one else," Mère Marie said eagerly. "He'd send his best troops to help us. And more colonists, too. But now, under the present circumstances—"

The Bishop sighed. "That's right, Mother. Under the present circumstances I must stay where I am and suffer with my flock."

The days passed, however, and no Iroquois appeared to storm Quebec. Indeed, by the first week in June, both religious and layfolk were in a state of nervous exhaustion. What evil scheme had the enemy in mind? For almost five weeks their great war canoes had been expected along the Saint Lawrence, yet now—

"Don't worry," a young farm worker told Mère Marie one day. "God won't let the Iroquois surprise us."

Mère Marie smiled wanly. "You think so, my son?"

The boy's eyes glowed. "I'm sure of it, Mère Marie. Just wait and see."

He was right. Early the next morning the watchdogs commenced a fearful barking in the garden as two ragged young Indians tried to scale the convent wall. "D-don't shoot!" begged the newcomers, as a dozen soldiers took instant aim with their guns. "W-we bring you g-good news..."

Suspicious of all strangers, the commander hurried forward to investigate. Then he nodded curtly. "It's all right," he told his men. "These boys are Christian Hurons from Montreal. Let them come in."

A moment later, the nuns and the soldiers were listening to an incredible tale. More than two weeks ago, said the Hurons, a resident of Montreal named Adam Dollard had grown tired of waiting for the Iroquois to strike. With De Maisonneuve's permission, he and sixteen other young men had set themselves up in a makeshift fort at Sault Saint Louis, along the Ottawa River, and had boldly challenged two Iroquois canoes that were coming downstream. Taken by surprise, the enemy had suffered terrible losses. However, a few had escaped to warn their comrades. Before long, five hundred savage Iroquois had been at the very walls of Dollard's little fort, goaded into fury at the knowledge that for once the French were gaining the upper hand.

The commander was amazed. "Seventeen Frenchmen against five hundred Iroquois?" he exclaimed. "Good heavens! Tell us more, my friends!"

Only after an embarrassed silence, however, could the youthful pair be persuaded to resume their story. Then they ruefully admitted that in the beginning Dollard had had far more than sixteen companions. Indeed, four Algonquins and forty

"D-DON'T SHOOT! W-WE BRING YOU
G-GOOD NEWS. . ."

Hurons, themselves included, had been with him. Eventually, though, all save the Huron chief and the four Algonquins had deserted to the Iroquois.

The commander frowned. "Seventeen Frenchmen, one Huron, four Algonquins—twenty-two men in all!" he snapped. "You mean you left these poor souls to their deaths?"

Trembling, the young Hurons lowered their heads and refused to answer the question. Nor was their confidence restored until Mère Marie, overcome with pity, brought them food and drink. "Don't be afraid," she urged gently. "Just tell us exactly what happened."

Still trembling, the Hurons obeyed. Adam Dollard and his twenty-one companions, they said, had fought for eight days and nights at Sault Saint Louis without losing a single man. At times, believing that the Great White Spirit must be with the Frenchmen in their little fort, the Iroquois had been ready to surrender. Yet in the end, on May 21, they had made one last desperate attack. Sensing their plans, Dollard had thrown a lighted powder keg over the wall. Alas! The keg had hit a tree. Bouncing backward, it had then exploded and destroyed the fort.

"The Iroquois found only three men still alive when they searched the ruins, Mother, but those three fought to the death. Before we escaped from the Iroquois, we saw how impressed their chiefs were by Dollard's stand. They kept insisting that if only seventeen Frenchmen could be so brave, the garrisons at Montreal and Quebec would surely be able to destroy the whole Iroquois nation. Now we've come to tell you they no longer plan to come here. You're safe, Mother, and so is everyone else."

There was joy in Quebec when the glorious news of Dollard's bravery had made the rounds. Promptly Bishop de Laval ordered a solemn *Te Deum* to be sung in every chapel, followed by special prayers for the heroes of Sault Saint Louis. Yet even as he prayed and rejoiced with his little flock, the Bishop was heavy-hearted. Something told him that the present peace would never last. The Iroquois were still a proud and savage race. Within a year or so, when younger men had replaced the fallen warriors, they would seek their revenge.

"If only I could go back to France and tell King Louis of our need for more troops," he reflected.

But it was not until the summer of 1662—by which time the Iroquois had killed two Sulpician priests at Montreal and also one of De Maisonneuve's best friends, Major Lambert Closse—that the Bishop was able to journey to the French court. Then, though King Louis XIV showed him every courtesy and promised substantial help for New France, four more years passed before a sizable French force under the Marquis Alexandre de Tracy had been assembled.

It was on September 14, 1666, that De Tracy and his men finally set out for Iroquois country—the northern part of the present-day state of New York. As the Ursulines watched the glittering ranks depart from Fort Saint Louis, they hoped that the efforts of this gallant band would not be in vain. True, Alexandre de Tracy was a brave and experienced soldier. His army of more than twelve hundred men was the largest ever seen in Canada. Nevertheless, difficult weeks were in store for both officers and men. A galling march of three hundred miles lay ahead—through the dense forests south of the Saint Lawrence, over mountains and across two large lakes. Worse still: unlike the Iroquois, the French could not go without food for days on end. They must carry a constant supply of provisions with them, as well as the usual quantities of arms and ammunition.

"Dear Father in Heaven, do give our troops the necessary strength!" begged Mère Marie. "Canada will surely be lost if they don't win out against the Iroquois. . ."

Others were of like mind, and for many days all Quebec stormed Heaven for the success of De Tracy's expedition. Finally, in late October, a breathless messenger brought word that the Iroquois had fled from the invading French with scarcely a struggle. Their hastily abandoned villages had been burned to the ground. Even now peace envoys were on the way to Quebec.

Somehow this news seemed too remarkable to be true. "But it *is* true!" one person told another excitedly. "More messengers are arriving at Fort Saint Louis who say the same thing! Isn't it wonderful that we will have peace at last?"

Still, Mère Marie's heart ached for those unbaptized Iroquois who had fallen in battle, for the women and children who must now face the winter cold without a home or supplies. However, she agreed with everyone else that De Tracy's victory was a blessing for the settlement, and in the end for the Indians themselves. Not since 1658, because of the bitter enmity between the Iroquois and the Hurons, had Jesuit missionaries been able to preach the Gospel in the vast wilderness south of the Saint Lawrence. Now, though, with the Iroquois finally ready to make peace with the French, and also with their Huron allies—

"The Jesuits will go to Iroquois country with the holy Catholic Faith once again," Mère Marie told herself happily. "Perhaps they'll even be able to send us some of the Iroquois children to educate in the knowledge and love of God."

CHAPTER 11

THE PASSING YEARS

MÈRE MARIE'S hopes were to be realized. Now the Iroquois were more than willing for several of their little girls to enter the Ursuline school in Quebec. Indeed, by 1669 the great chief himself, Garakontié, had become so interested in the Faith that he was asking to be baptized. The ceremony, performed by Bishop de Laval, finally took place before an admiring crowd in the cathedral of Quebec. And to Garakontié's great joy, Governor Daniel de Courcelles acted as his godfather.

"Well, time has certainly changed things here," the Bishop told Mère Marie, when next he visited the convent. "It seems only yesterday that I arrived in Quebec. Yet that was all of ten years ago."

Mère Marie smiled. "It's all of thirty years since I came, Monseigneur. And Quebec? It was only a poor little village then, with scarcely two hundred people. Now, thanks to you, it's a busy and bustling town of nearly a thousand souls."

The Bishop's eyes shot open with astonishment.

"Thanks to *me*, Mother?"

"Yes, Monseigneur, thanks to you. After all, where would we be if you hadn't returned to France seven years ago and explained our needs to King Louis? Certainly he'd never have sent the good De Tracy to help us. Or have taken such a personal interest in the colony himself. Ah, Monseigneur, without you our work here could never have lasted!"

For a moment the Bishop was thoughtful. Then he shrugged and smiled. "You're forgetting all the help I've had, Mother, not only from yourselves, the Ursulines, but from all the good priests and nuns who've been laboring here in New France. And I've had prayers, too—the prayers of saints, I'm sure. For instance, just think of little Mère Catherine de Saint Augustin, who died last year when she was only thirty-six!"

Mère Marie's dark eyes sparkled. "You really believe Mère Catherine was a saint, Monseigneur?"

The Bishop nodded vigorously. "Yes, Mother, I really do. Even more. I'm convinced that someday the Church in Canada will try to bring about her canonization."

Long after Bishop de Laval had taken his departure, Mère Marie sat pondering these words. Mère Catherine de Saint Augustin! Why, it seemed only yesterday that the pretty little hospital nun had been encouraging her to be of good heart after that dreadful night of December 30, 1650..."*You mustn't feel too bad about the fire, Mother. After all, the sufferings it brought are only part of God's plan.*

*I know they'll win many blessings for your commu-
nity in the years ahead. Just wait and see."*

The minutes passed, and still Mère Marie sat lost
in thought. Had God blessed Mère Catherine with
the grace to see into the future, she asked herself.
Oh, surely so! Certainly in later life Mère Catherine
had often read the secrets of men's hearts, even
nursed the incurable back to health. Indeed, who
could tell the number of her charities? Or the
extent to which she had offered herself as a victim
for the souls in New France?

"Yes, my dear, I do believe you went straight to
Heaven when you died," said Mère Marie, finally
rousing herself for the many tasks that lay at hand.
"Oh, please don't forget us, now that you're so
happy! Quebec still needs your prayers so very
much . . ."

The Ursulines agreed with Mère Marie. Quebec
did need prayers, especially for the success of the
Bishop's new seminary, the first house of its kind
in North America where young men could study
for the priesthood. Then there were "the King's
Girls," those carefully selected young women whom
His Majesty was now sending out from France each
year to become wives for the colonists. Surely they
needed special grace and strength in order to make
good Catholic homes in the New World. Finally
there were the colonists themselves, particularly
the misguided souls among them who still persisted
in giving French wines and brandies to the Indians
for the beaver skins which they brought home from
the hunt.

"How terrible that is!" Mère Marie told Mère Marguerite de Saint Athanase one day in March 1670. "The Indians love alcohol so much, yet after a mere taste or two they become like madmen. Even our best converts are then no better than their pagan brothers."

Mère Marguerite sighed and shook her head. "I know. The Indians aren't able to touch alcohol without doing the most dreadful things. Wouldn't you think that our colonists would respect this fact, and not tempt the poor souls as they do? But no. They want plenty of beaver skins to send back to France, so they can make fortunes for themselves. Even the Bishop's threat to excommunicate them for leading the Indians into sin counts for little with them."

Mère Marie hesitated. Then, a faint smile upon her lips, she looked fondly at Mère Marguerite. "I've prayed and thought about the liquor question for years," she said slowly. "And other problems, too. Somehow I don't seem able to cope with them as I used to do. Do you know what I've decided?"

"No, Mother. I can't imagine."

"Well, I've decided on a very important step. Just listen to what I have in mind, my dear—for you and for me!..."

The next day there was startling news for everyone in Quebec. Mère Marie had asked the community not to elect her as superior again. She had also asked to be released from her present duties. And though both requests had been granted and she was being succeeded by Mère Marguerite de Saint

Athanase, a holy and experienced nun whom everyone loved, there was reason to be alarmed. From
all accounts, Mère Marie had retired from office not
only because of advancing years but also because
of poor health. She was even convinced that her
days on earth were numbered.

"Do tell me that's not so, Mère Cécile!" begged
Madame d'Ailleboust, widow of the third Governor
of New France, who came hurrying to the convent
as soon as she had heard the news. "Good heavens,
I've known Mère Marie for almost twenty-seven
years—ever since I came to Canada! In all that time
she's worked so tirelessly for others that I just took
it for granted she had the best of health."

Mère Cécile nodded. "I understand, Madame.
We've all been taking Mère Marie for granted, more
or less. But now—"

"Then it is true? The poor soul isn't well?"

"She's not at all well, Madame. Although she
never mentioned them to anyone, she's been having
spells of weakness for many months. And great
pain, too."

"Heavens! Do the doctors know what's wrong?"

"Not yet, although they're hoping it may be just
a case of simple exhaustion. After all, Mère Marie
is no longer a young woman. She'll be seventy-one
years old next October 28."

"I know. And she's never tried to make things
easy for herself."

"Never. Still, with rest and nourishing food, she
may be quite herself by the time summer comes."

Early in June of that same year, 1670, many people were convinced that God had answered their prayers for Mère Marie. Though she was still far from well, she was certainly not an invalid. Nor would she allow herself to be treated as one. True, the occasional spells of weakness persisted, with their accompanying aches and pains, but they were not really serious, she said. They were just part of growing old. Perhaps Mère Marguerite would permit her to have a few light duties about the house, such as hearing the children's catechism, writing community business letters home to France and helping the younger nuns to learn the Indian languages?

"Well, I think that would be all right," said Mère Marguerite, relieved that her good friend seemed to be holding her own. "Just don't tire yourself, Mother. That's all I ask."

The teaching of the Indian languages was a task especially dear to Mère Marie. She had never forgotten her own difficulties when she had begun to study Huron years before. What an impossible chore it had seemed then! The cumbersome words and phrases which the little Indian girls had tossed off so freely had been like so many heavy stones rolling about inside her head. Yet God had been good. He had enabled her to learn Huron in less than three months. He had also permitted her to master Montagnais, Algonquin and Iroquois. Indeed, the day had finally come when she was compiling dictionaries and prayerbooks in these difficult tongues and translating the catechism and large portions of the Sacred Scriptures as well.

"There's just no one like Mère Marie when it comes to languages," Governor Daniel de Courcelles told his adviser, Monsieur Jean Talon, as they sat in conference one day. "She's still a real scholar in spite of her age and infirmities. The nuns and the children are fortunate to have her with them."

Monsieur Talon nodded. "I know. And from all accounts her son's a scholar, too."

"Dom Claude? He is indeed, and more than that. Two years ago he was made assistant superior general of the Benedictines of Saint Maur—the second most important post in the congregation."

"How wonderful!"

"More wonderful than you think. Did you know that Dom Claude was once just a shiftless lad who couldn't settle down to anything? When he was thirteen, for instance, the Jesuits dismissed him from their school in Rennes. Later on, when he wanted to study for the priesthood in the Society of Jesus, they turned him down pointblank."

"The good men were doubtful of his vocation?"

"Very doubtful."

"They must have forgotten the power of a mother's prayers."

"That is so, Monsieur. Even as a young woman, Mère Marie had asked God to let her be a victim for Claude's failings. Finally He blessed that request. Only on the Last Day will we know the martyrdom that she suffered in order to win her son's conversion."

Bishop de Laval was also familiar with Dom Claude's unusual life story. In fact, every day he begged God's blessing on Mère Marie's priest son. Even more. On his various pilgrimages to Saint Anne's shrine at Beaupré, a pretty little village some twenty miles east of Quebec, he remembered him in prayer.

"How I love Saint Anne's shrine!" the Bishop told Mère Marie one bright April morning in the year 1671, when he had stopped at the convent to visit the nuns and to give them his blessing. "I surely find it easier to pray there than anywhere else."

Mère Marie's dark eyes were alight. She was feeling so much better today, possibly because of the Bishop's visit. And though the Rule did not permit her to leave her cloister even for a pilgrimage to Saint Anne's shrine, she was well aware of the many wonders that had been taking place there since March 13, 1658, when a poor cripple named Louis Guimont had been suddenly cured after praying to the mother of the Blessed Virgin.

"You went to Beaupré for a special reason, Monseigneur?" she asked.

The Bishop nodded. "I did, Mother. I went to ask Saint Anne's blessing on the trip to France which I hope to make this year. We have a new Pope now, you know, Clement X. And His Majesty—well, there seem to be difficulties between the French court and the Vatican over the future of the Church in Canada. I've asked Saint Anne to bring everything to a happy conclusion. Besides all that, four new Ursulines should be arriving here in September. I've asked Saint Anne to bless them in every

"I WENT TO ASK ST. ANNE'S BLESSING ON THE TRIP
TO FRANCE WHICH I HOPE TO MAKE THIS YEAR."

way. And you, too, Mother, that you may have better health."

What a kindly man the Bishop was, thought Mère Marie, how thoughtful of everyone. "That was very good of you, Monseigneur," she said earnestly. "I . . . I really don't know how to thank you."

"Don't try, Mère Marie. Just pray that my trip will be a success. There are some very important things to settle, you know."

Mère Marie smiled. "Of course, Monseigneur. All of us will miss you while you're away—I am thinking particularly of Madame de la Peltrie."

"Please give Madame de la Peltrie my respectful compliments," said the Bishop, rising to leave. "No one has given more generously of her fortune and talents to build the future generations of New France."

Alas! Shortly after the Bishop's departure for France in early November, Marie Madeleine de la Peltrie caught a severe cold. Though she was given every care, pleurisy soon set in and she was dead by November 18.

"It can't be!" people told one another incredulously. "Why, only last week Madame de la Peltrie was teaching the little Indian girls their prayers!"

"And making plans for their Christmas party!"

"She wasn't so very old either."

"Why, no. Just sixty-nine."

A month later there was more cause for concern. Mère Marie had suffered a sudden relapse, and was now afflicted with several painful abscesses. No medicine seemed to help. Indeed, by late January of 1672, when it was decided that she must receive the Last Sacraments, the Ursulines scarcely knew what to do.

"First Madame de la Peltrie, now Mère Marie," they said to one another, sorrowing. "It's almost too much to bear. . ."

Père Jérôme Lalemant agreed. The community could ill afford to lose its two foundresses within a matter of a few weeks. "We must pray as we've never prayed before," he told the nuns. "The good God knows how much we need to keep Mère Marie with us."

So everyone began to pray to the Sacred Heart of Jesus, as Mère Marie had always urged them to do whenever they wished a special favor from Heaven. This beautiful devotion (which twenty-four-year-old Soeur Marguerite Marie Alacoque had not yet introduced into her Visitation monastery in Paray-le-Monial, France) brought great peace to the troubled nuns. How consoling to remember those wonderful words: *Ask Me by the Heart of Jesus, My most beloved Son. Through Him I will hear you and grant you your requests.*

"Now everything's going to be all right," Soeur Saint Laurent told Mère Marguerite one night. "Even if Mère Marie should leave us, we'll be given the strength to make God's will our own. And that's all that matters, isn't it?"

Mère Marguerite brushed back her tears. "Of course, my dear," she said, smiling bravely. "That's all that matters."

In spite of the many prayers, however, and the

best of care, Mère Marie grew steadily weaker.
Indeed, by late March she knew that her time on
earth was short.

"How I wish I could see the children again!" she
told Mère Marguerite one night, when she found
it impossible to sleep. "Do. . .do you think it could
be arranged?"

Mère Marguerite scarcely knew what to say. How
pale her good friend looked, how worn with pain.
And yet—

"Of course," she said comfortingly, "if it wouldn't
tire you."

Mère Marie smiled. "Children have never tired
me, Mother. I. . .I love them too much."

So the next day a number of little French and
Indian girls were excused from their classes and
brought to visit Mère Marie. But they were ill at
ease as Soeur Saint Laurent led them into the sick-
room. How terrible that Mère Marie was dying!
That in a little while she would be put into a deep
hole and covered with cold, wet earth!

"There, now, a grave isn't anything to worry
about," said Mère Marie, reading the children's
thoughts and summoning all her strength to speak
up clearly and to be cheerful. "Didn't you know
that it's only a place for—well, for old clothes?"

Eight-year-old Pauline stared in awed silence.
Then suddenly she found her tongue. "Old
clothes!" she burst out incredulously. "But. . .but
I thought. . ."

Mère Marie shook her head. "A grave is for old
clothes, my dear. Listen, and I'll try to explain."

Slowly and painfully Mère Marie lifted her hands. Weren't these hands worn and stiff? she asked the children. No longer able to work? Of course! And so was the rest of her seventy-one-year-old body. But the soul within? The real Mère Marie? Ah, that was ageless! It could never die. In a little while, when God would call the soul to Himself, it would be only too glad to shed its old clothes, the body, and have everything buried neatly in a grave.

"And why will that be, my dears?"

The children hesitated. "Because the soul is seeing God for the first time, Mother?" suggested nine-year-old Annette timidly. "Because now it wants only Him?"

Mère Marie smiled and nodded. "That's it. That's exactly it. But there's something else to remember, too. Can anyone tell me what it is?"

Suddenly the children were no longer afraid. "I know, Mère Marie!" exclaimed ten-year-old Hélène eagerly. "It's about God's friends. On the Last Day there'll be the most wonderful miracle for them. All at once their bodies will be nice and new."

"Their souls will go back into their bodies and never leave them again."

"After that, they won't ever be tired or sick any more."

"It'll be nice weather all the time."

"Without any troubles or worries."

"Forever and ever and ever!"

Slowly tears of happiness began to fill Mère Marie's dark eyes. How wonderful that the children understood! And if only she could speak longer with them. But her strength was almost gone. She was tired...so very tired...and Soeur Saint Laurent seemed to be taking the children away...

"Maybe...maybe tomorrow they can come again," she thought. "Truly, they're my heart's delight..."

The children did come again the next day. And the next and the next. But soon Mère Marie no longer had the strength to speak with them, or even to bless them as they gathered about her bed. Indeed, late in the afternoon of April 29, when she had received the Last Sacraments for still another time, everyone realized that the end was near.

"My dear, haven't you a little message for Dom Claude?" asked Mère Marguerite, bending anxiously over the bed and taking her good friend's hand in hers. "We'll be writing to him, you know, when the ships come in."

Slowly Mère Marie stirred and opened her eyes. The pain was bad now, so very bad! She could do little but press a crucifix to her lips.

"T-tell him that in my h-heart I...I bear him to Heaven!" she gasped. "T-tell him that I will p-pray for him to be a...a saint!"

Mère Marguerite choked back a sob. How Mère Marie was suffering! And not for herself, but for the work to which she had given her life—the conversion of souls in the New World, especially the souls of the young.

Tears in her eyes, she turned to Mère Cécile. "Surely this is the end?" she whispered. "Surely she can't last much longer?"

But twenty-four hours passed, and still Mère Marie continued to cling to life. Then late in the afternoon of April 30, the community began the prayers for the dying once again:

May the heavens be opened to her, may the Angels rejoice with her. Receive Thy handmaid, O Lord, into Thy Kingdom. Let Saint Michael, the Archangel of God, who is the chief of the heavenly host, conduct her. Let the holy Angels of God come forth to meet her, and bring her into the holy city of Jerusalem. . .

As six o'clock struck, Mère Marie stirred and sighed, and the crucifix dropped from her fingers. Far to the west, the April sun slipped briefly through the clouds to bathe in sudden splendor the great rock of Quebec.

HISTORICAL NOTE
Added by the Publisher, 1994

Marie of the Incarnation was beatified in 1980 by Pope John Paul II.

Her son, Dom Claude Martin, is said to have died in the odor of sanctity when he passed from this world in 1696. He wrote the first biography of his mother.

The Ursuline Blessed Marie of the Incarnation (1599-1672) who is the subject of this book is not to be confused with another Blessed Marie of the Incarnation (1566-1618), of Paris, who, as a wife and mother of six children, established the Carmelite Order in France. Her name in the world was Madame Barbe Acarie. For a brief period she was directed by St. Francis de Sales. After her husband's death, Madame Acarie entered Carmel as a lay sister, taking the name Marie of the Incarnation. At her death there were fourteen houses of the Carmelite Order in France. She was beatified in 1791.

By the same author . . .

6 GREAT CATHOLIC
BOOKS FOR CHILDREN

. . . and for all young people ages 10 to 100!!

1137 THE CHILDREN OF FATIMA—And Our Lady's Message to the World. 162 pp. PB. 15 Illus. Impr. The wonderful story of Our Lady's appearances to little Jacinta, Francisco and Lucia at Fatima in 1917.   8.00

1138 THE CURÉ OF ARS—The Story of St. John Vianney, Patron Saint of Parish Priests. 211 pp. PB. 38 Illus. Impr. The many adventures that met young St. John Vianney when he set out to become a priest.   12.00

1139 THE LITTLE FLOWER—The Story of St. Therese of the Child Jesus. 167 pp. PB. 24 Illus. Impr. Tells what happened when little Therese decided to become a saint.   8.00

1140 PATRON SAINT OF FIRST COMMUNICANTS—The Story of Blessed Imelda Lambertini. 85 pp. PB. 14 Illus. Impr. Tells of the wonderful miracle God worked to answer little Imelda's prayer.   6.00

1141 THE MIRACULOUS MEDAL—The Story of Our Lady's Appearances to St. Catherine Labouré. 107 pp. PB. 21 Illus. Impr. The beautiful story of what happened when young Sister Catherine saw Our Lady.   7.00

1142 ST. LOUIS DE MONTFORT—The Story of Our Lady's Slave. 211 pp. PB. 20 Illus. Impr. The remarkable story of the priest who went around helping people become "slaves" of Jesus through Mary.   12.00

1136 ALL 6 BOOKS ABOVE (Reg. 53.00)   THE SET: 43.00

Prices subject to change.

U.S. & CAN. POST./HDLG.: $1-$10, add $2; $10.01-$20, add $3;
$20.01-$30, add $4; $30.01-$50, add $5; $50.01-$75, add $6; $75.01-up, add $7.

At your Bookdealer or direct from the Publisher.
Call Toll Free 1-800-437-5876

Also by the same author . . .

6 <u>MORE</u> GREAT CATHOLIC BOOKS FOR CHILDREN
. . . and for all young people ages 10 to 100!!

1200 SAINT THOMAS AQUINAS—The Story of "The Dumb Ox." 81 pp. PB. 16 Illus. Impr. The remarkable story of how St. Thomas, called in school "The Dumb Ox," became the greatest Catholic teacher ever.   6.00

1201 SAINT CATHERINE OF SIENA—The Story of the Girl Who Saw Saints in the Sky. 65 pp. PB. 13 Illus. The amazing life of the most famous Catherine in the history of the Church.   5.00

1202 SAINT HYACINTH OF POLAND—The Story of The Apostle of the North. 189 pp. PB. 16 Illus. Impr. Shows how the holy Catholic Faith came to Poland, Lithuania, Prussia, Scandinavia and Russia.   11.00

1203 SAINT MARTIN DE PORRES—The Story of The Little Doctor of Lima, Peru. 122 pp. PB. 16 Illus. Impr. The incredible life and miracles of this black boy who became a great saint.   7.00

1204 SAINT ROSE OF LIMA—The Story of The First Canonized Saint of the Americas. 132 pp. PB. 13 Illus. Impr. The remarkable life of the little Rose of South America.   8.00

1205 PAULINE JARICOT—Foundress of the Living Rosary and The Society for the Propagation of the Faith. 244 pp. PB. 21 Illus. Impr. The story of a rich young girl and her many spiritual adventures.   13.00

1206 ALL 6 BOOKS ABOVE (Reg. 50.00)   THE SET: 40.00

Prices subject to change.

U.S. & CAN. POST./HDLG.: $1-$10, add $2; $10.01-$20, add $3; $20.01-$30, add $4; $30.01-$50, add $5; $50.01-$75, add $6; $75.01-up, add $7.

At your Bookdealer or direct from the Publisher.
Call Toll Free 1-800-437-5876

More books by the same author . . .

<u>8 MORE</u> GREAT CATHOLIC
BOOKS FOR CHILDREN
. . . and for all young people ages 10 to 100!!

1230 SAINT PAUL THE APOSTLE—The Story of the Apostle to the Gentiles. 231 pp. PB. 23 Illus. Impr. The many adventures that met St. Paul in the early Catholic Church.   13.00

1231 SAINT BENEDICT—The Story of the Father of the Western Monks. 158 pp. PB. 19 Illus. Impr. The life and great miracles of the man who planted monastic life in Europe.   8.00

1232 SAINT MARGARET MARY—And the Promises of the Sacred Heart of Jesus. 224 pp. PB. 21 Illus. Impr. The wonderful story of remarkable gifts from Heaven. Includes St. Claude de la Colombière.   11.00

1233 SAINT DOMINIC—Preacher of the Rosary and Founder of the Dominican Order. 156 pp. PB. 19 Illus. Impr. The miracles, trials and travels of one of the Church's most famous saints.   8.00

Continued on next page . . .

**At your Bookdealer or direct from the Publisher.
Call Toll Free 1-800-437-5876**

1234 KING DAVID AND HIS SONGS—A Story of the Psalms. 138 pp. PB. 23 Illus. Impr. The story of the shepherd boy who became a warrior, a hero, a fugitive, a king, and more.   8.00

1235 SAINT FRANCIS SOLANO—Wonder-Worker of the New World and Apostle of Argentina and Peru. 205 pp. PB. 19 Illus. Impr. The story of St. Francis' remarkable deeds in Spain and South America.   11.00

1236 SAINT JOHN MASIAS—Marvelous Dominican Gatekeeper of Lima, Peru. 156 pp. PB. 14 Illus. Impr. The humble brother who fought the devil and freed a million souls from Purgatory.   8.00

1237 BLESSED MARIE OF NEW FRANCE—The Story of the First Missionary Sisters in Canada. 152 pp. PB. 18 Illus. Impr. The story of a wife, mother and nun—and her many adventures in pioneer Canada.   9.00

1238 ALL 8 BOOKS ABOVE (Reg. 76.00)   THE SET: 60.00

Prices subject to change.

Get the Complete Set!! . . .

SET OF ALL 20 TITLES

by Mary Fabyan Windeatt

(Individually priced—179.00   Reg. set prices—143.00)

1256 THE SET OF ALL 20 . . . . Only 125.00

U.S. & CAN. POST./HDLG.: $1-$10, add $2; $10.01-$20, add $3; $20.01-$30, add $4; $30.01-$50, add $5; $50.01-$75, add $6; $75.01-up, add $7.

**At your Bookdealer or direct from the Publisher.
Call Toll Free 1-800-437-5876**

TAN BOOKS AND PUBLISHERS, INC.
P.O. Box 424
Rockford, Illinois 61105